AMERICAN POLITICAL, ECONOMIC, AND SECURITY ISSUES

FLOATING RATE NOTES

ANALYSIS OF TREASURY'S NEWEST DEBT MANAGEMENT SECURITY

AMERICAN POLITICAL, ECONOMIC, AND SECURITY ISSUES

Additional books in this series can be found on Nova's website under the Series tab.

Additional e-books in this series can be found on Nova's website under the e-book tab.

AMERICAN POLITICAL, ECONOMIC, AND SECURITY ISSUES

FLOATING RATE NOTES

ANALYSIS OF TREASURY'S NEWEST DEBT MANAGEMENT SECURITY

ROSALYN MERCER
EDITOR

New York

Copyright © 2014 by Nova Science Publishers, Inc.

All rights reserved. No part of this book may be reproduced, stored in a retrieval system or transmitted in any form or by any means: electronic, electrostatic, magnetic, tape, mechanical photocopying, recording or otherwise without the written permission of the Publisher.

For permission to use material from this book please contact us:
Telephone 631-231-7269; Fax 631-231-8175
Web Site: http://www.novapublishers.com

NOTICE TO THE READER

The Publisher has taken reasonable care in the preparation of this book, but makes no expressed or implied warranty of any kind and assumes no responsibility for any errors or omissions. No liability is assumed for incidental or consequential damages in connection with or arising out of information contained in this book. The Publisher shall not be liable for any special, consequential, or exemplary damages resulting, in whole or in part, from the readers' use of, or reliance upon, this material. Any parts of this book based on government reports are so indicated and copyright is claimed for those parts to the extent applicable to compilations of such works.

Independent verification should be sought for any data, advice or recommendations contained in this book. In addition, no responsibility is assumed by the publisher for any injury and/or damage to persons or property arising from any methods, products, instructions, ideas or otherwise contained in this publication.

This publication is designed to provide accurate and authoritative information with regard to the subject matter covered herein. It is sold with the clear understanding that the Publisher is not engaged in rendering legal or any other professional services. If legal or any other expert assistance is required, the services of a competent person should be sought. FROM A DECLARATION OF PARTICIPANTS JOINTLY ADOPTED BY A COMMITTEE OF THE AMERICAN BAR ASSOCIATION AND A COMMITTEE OF PUBLISHERS.

Additional color graphics may be available in the e-book version of this book.

Library of Congress Cataloging-in-Publication Data

ISBN: 978-1-63463-214-0

Published by Nova Science Publishers, Inc. † New York

CONTENTS

Preface		**vii**
Chapter 1	Debt Management: Floating Rate Notes Can Help Treasury Meet Borrowing Goals, but Additional Actions Are Needed to Help Manage Risk *United States Government Accountability Office*	**1**
Chapter 2	How Treasury Issues Debt *Mindy R. Levit*	**49**
Index		**75**

PREFACE

Issuing floating rate notes (FRN) is likely to help the Department of the Treasury (Treasury) meet its goals to borrow at the lowest cost over time, extend the average maturity of the debt portfolio, and increase demand for Treasury securities, but it also presents risks related to changes in interest rates. This book evaluates Treasury's rationale for introducing FRNs and identifies the demand for Treasury securities from a broad range of investors to assess whether changes would help Treasury meet its goals.

Chapter 1 - To continue meeting its goal of financing the federal government's borrowing needs at the lowest cost over time, Treasury began issuing a new type of security—a 2-year floating rate note (FRN)—in January 2014. The FRN pays interest at a rate that resets periodically based on changes in the rate of the 13-week Treasury bill (to which the FRN is indexed). GAO was asked to review Treasury debt management, including this product and other debt management issues.

This report (1) evaluates Treasury's rationale for introducing FRNs and (2) identifies the demand for Treasury securities from a broad range of investors to assess whether changes would help Treasury meet its goals. To address these objectives, GAO used Treasury auction data from 1980 -2014 to simulate the costs of Treasury FRNs, reviewed Treasury documents, surveyed a non-generalizable sample of 82 large domestic institutional investors across sectors, and interviewed market participants and academic experts. (For the survey and results, see GAO-14-562SP.)

Chapter 2 - The U.S. Department of the Treasury (Treasury), among other roles, manages the country's debt. The primary objective of Treasury's debt management strategy is to finance the government's borrowing needs at the lowest cost over time. To accomplish this Treasury adheres to three principles:

(1) to issue debt in a regular and predictable pattern, (2) to provide transparency in the decision-making process, and (3) to seek continuous improvements in the auction process.

Specifically, the Office of Debt Management (ODM) makes all decisions related to debt issuance and the management of the United States debt portfolio. When federal spending exceeds revenues, the ODM directs the Bureau of Public Debt (BPD) to borrow the funds needed to finance government operations by selling securities to the public and government agencies via an auction process. BPD manages the operational aspects of the issuance of Treasury securities, including the systems related to and the monitoring of the auction process.

During the mid-1970s, Treasury faced a period of rising nominal federal budget deficits and debt requiring unanticipated increases in issuances of securities. At that time, debt management was characterized by an ad-hoc, offering-by-offering survey of market participants. Due to the lack of transparency in such a process and the potential for market related volatility, a new strategy was implemented in order to provide greater transparency and regularity to the debt management process. The purpose of this new strategy was to modernize the Treasury securities market, to realize the benefits of predictability in an environment of large deficits, and to use this predictability to induce policymakers to alter the practices of the institutions they managed. Treasury auctions became a key part of the new strategy focusing on regular and predictable debt management.

Most of the debt sold by the federal government is marketable, meaning that the securities can be resold on the secondary market. Currently, Treasury offers four types of marketable securities: Treasury bills, notes, bonds, and inflation protected securities (TIPS), sold in over 250 auctions per year. A small portion of debt held by the public and nearly all intragovernmental debt (debt held by government trust funds) is nonmarketable.

Investors examine several key factors when deciding whether they should purchase Treasury securities, including price, expected return, and risk. Treasury securities provide a known stream of income and offer greater liquidity than other types of fixed-income securities. Because they are also backed by the full faith and credit of the United States, they are often seen as one of the safest investments available, though investors are not totally immune from losses. Prices are determined by investors who place a value on Treasury securities based on these characteristics.

Legislative activity can affect Treasury's ability to issue debt and can impact the budget process. Congress sets a statutory limit on federal debt levels in an effort to assert its constitutional prerogatives to control spending and impose a form of fiscal accountability. The statutory limit on the debt can constrain debt operations, which, in the past, has hampered traditional practices when the limit was approached. The accounting of asset purchases in the federal budget has created differences between how much debt Treasury has to borrow to make those purchases and how much the same purchases will impact the budget deficit. If budget deficits continue to rise, thereby causing more resources to be devoted to paying interest on the debt, there will be fewer funds

In: Floating Rate Notes
Editor: Rosalyn Mercer

ISBN: 978-1-63463-214-0
© 2014 Nova Science Publishers, Inc.

Chapter 1

DEBT MANAGEMENT: FLOATING RATE NOTES CAN HELP TREASURY MEET BORROWING GOALS, BUT ADDITIONAL ACTIONS ARE NEEDED TO HELP MANAGE RISK[*]

United States Government Accountability Office

WHY GAO DID THIS STUDY

To continue meeting its goal of financing the federal government's borrowing needs at the lowest cost over time, Treasury began issuing a new type of security—a 2-year floating rate note (FRN)—in January 2014. The FRN pays interest at a rate that resets periodically based on changes in the rate of the 13-week Treasury bill (to which the FRN is indexed). GAO was asked to review Treasury debt management, including this product and other debt management issues.

This report (1) evaluates Treasury's rationale for introducing FRNs and (2) identifies the demand for Treasury securities from a broad range of investors to assess whether changes would help Treasury meet its goals. To address these objectives, GAO used Treasury auction data from 1980 -2014 to

---

[*] This is an edited, reformatted and augmented version of the United States Government Accountability Office publication, GAO-14-535, dated June 2014.

simulate the costs of Treasury FRNs, reviewed Treasury documents, surveyed a non-generalizable sample of 82 large domestic institutional investors across sectors, and interviewed market participants and academic experts. (For the survey and results, see GAO-14-562SP.)

WHAT GAO RECOMMENDS

GAO recommends that Treasury (1) track and report a measure of interest rate risk in its debt portfolio, (2) analyze the price effects of the difference between the term of the index rate and the reset period, (3) examine opportunities for additional new types of securities, such as FRNs of other maturities, and (4) expand outreach to certain market participants. Treasury agreed with the recommendations and said that they had already taken steps to begin implementing them.

WHAT GAO FOUND

Issuing floating rate notes (FRN) is likely to help the Department of the Treasury (Treasury) meet its goals to borrow at the lowest cost over time, extend the average maturity of the debt portfolio, and increase demand for Treasury securities, but it also presents risks related to changes in interest rates.

GAO simulated the costs of 2-year Treasury FRNs using historical Treasury auction data and found that interest costs of the FRNs were generally less than costs of fixed-rate 2-year notes, but could be either more or less than costs of 13-week bills, depending on assumptions about how investors price the FRNs. GAO also found that in rising interest rate environments, the FRNs may be more costly than these alternatives.

Multiple components contribute to achieving lowest cost financing over time: issuing FRNs is part of Treasury's approach to achieving this goal. GAO analysis identified a number of design elements that may affect how FRNs contribute to that goal. Treasury officials believe it is prudent for Treasury to extend the average maturity of its debt portfolio because the debt level is already high and is expected to grow. Relative to issuing shorter-term debt, 2-year FRNs will help Treasury extend the average maturity of the debt portfolio and thereby reduce the risk inherent in going to market. Because the interest rate on a FRN can change during the life of the security, FRNs expose Treasury to the risk of rising interest rates whereas fixed-rate securities of the same maturity do not. These shifts in risk are likely to be small because currently FRNs are expected to constitute a small proportion of Treasury debt. Although managing interest rate risk is an important aspect of Treasury's goal to borrow at the lowest cost over time, Treasury does not track and report a measure of the average maturity of the portfolio that captures the additional interest rate risk of FRNs.

One element of the design of the 2-year FRN—the difference between the term of its index rate (13 weeks) and the length of its effective reset period (one week)—is not typical for floating rate notes and creates tradeoffs in interest rate risks but also may result in additional demand for the product. The risks could affect the pricing of FRNs and raise Treasury's borrowing costs in environments of high and volatile interest rates. Treasury officials told us they examined design elements, including this difference, before issuing the 2-year FRN. However, Treasury had not analyzed how the difference may affect FRN pricing.

FRNs give Treasury debt managers additional flexibility by increasing demand for Treasury securities and by adding a new security that meets the high demand for short-term securities. Results from GAO's survey of a broad range of investors and interviews with market participants found that market participants likely will purchase Treasury FRNs primarily as a substitute for other Treasury securities, but they will also purchase the FRNs as a substitute for non-Treasury securities, bringing new and potentially growing demand to Treasury. To provide the lowest cost of financing the government over time, Treasury must consider investor demand for new and existing products. Survey respondents indicated an interest in FRNs of additional maturities and in other new Treasury products. Treasury currently offers many ways for market participants to provide input, but GAO's survey identified opportunities for Treasury to enhance input from some sectors—including state and local government retirement fund managers.

ABBREVIATIONS

CMT	Constant Maturity Treasuries
FRBNY	Federal Reserve Bank of New York
FRN	floating rate note
GSE	government-sponsored enterprise

RMSE	root mean square error
TBAC	Treasury Borrowing Advisory Committee
TIPS	Treasury Inflation-Protected Securities
Treasury	Department of the Treasury
WAM	weighted average maturity

****

June 16, 2014

The Honorable Dave Camp
Chairman, Committee on Ways and Means
House of Representatives

Dear Mr. Chairman:

The U.S. Treasury market is the deepest and most liquid government debt market in the world, and throughout history the Department of the Treasury (Treasury) has been able to borrow the money it needs to finance the federal government. In recent years federal debt held by the public has risen dramatically, more than tripling in 10 years, from $3.9 trillion at the end of fiscal year 2003 to $12 trillion at the end of fiscal year 2013.[1] The economic slowdown and global financial crisis that contributed to this recent, rapid run-up in debt also brought about regulatory changes and a "flight to quality": this increased the demand for Treasury securities and helped keep the interest rates that Treasury paid to its investors near historic lows. Low rates meant that, while the debt more than tripled, the interest expense on Federal debt held by the public increased by only 58 percent from fiscal year 2003 through 2013 to $248 billion. But with debt projected to continue to grow and interest rates expected to rise, this cost will increase.

To continue to meet its goal of financing the federal government's borrowing needs at the lowest cost over time, in 2013 Treasury announced that for the first time in more than 15 years, it would begin issuing a new type of security—a Treasury floating rate note (FRN). FRNs differ from Treasury's traditional fixed-rate notes in that the FRNs pay interest at a rate that can rise and fall during the life of the security.

According to Treasury officials, FRNs will help Treasury to (1) borrow at the lowest cost over time, (2) increase the maturity profile of the debt portfolio, and (3) expand Treasury's investor base by attracting new buyers.

Debt Management 5

Floating Rate Note (FRN)

An FRN pays interest at a rate that is indexed to another rate, which can rise and fall during the life of the FRN. Treasury's 2-year FRN is indexed to the rate from Treasury's most-recent 13-week bill auction.

You asked us to review Treasury debt management in the context of its growing debt portfolio, including the introduction of FRNs. The objectives of this report are to (1) evaluate Treasury's rationale for introducing FRNs and (2) identify the demand for Treasury securities from a broad range of investors to determine whether changes would help Treasury meet its goals. To address these objectives, we did the following:

- Simulated the costs of 2-year FRNs, based on Treasury auction data from 1980 to 2014 using two models, each with different assumptions about the interest rates that Treasury would pay on the FRNs. We compared those costs to Treasury's actual costs of funding with 13-week bills and 2-year notes. We also analyzed how those costs varied over different interest rate environments. For more information on our cost simulations, see appendix I.
- Reviewed the analysis Treasury conducted in developing the 2-year FRN and the input Treasury received from market participants.
- Administered an online survey to 82 (62 completed the survey) of the largest domestic institutional holders of Treasury securities in the following sectors: money market mutual fund managers, mutual and exchange-traded fund managers, state and local government retirement fund managers, retail and commercial banks, life insurance providers, property-casualty insurance providers, and securities broker-dealers. Respondents were selected to achieve 50 percent of the total amount of Treasury holdings for each sector. The survey results are not generalizable to all investors in Treasury securities. For more information on our survey methodology, see appendix II. For aggregate survey results reproduced as an e-supplement, see GAO-14-562SP.
- Interviewed market participants—including six primary dealers and four asset managers—regarding the market for FRNs, the structure of FRNs, other actions Treasury could consider to expand demand for Treasury securities, and opportunities for investors to provide input to

Treasury.[2] We selected primary dealers and asset managers based on their holdings of Treasury securities and their public comments on Treasury's FRN proposals. The views expressed in these interviews are not generalizable to all market participants. Finally, we also interviewed five academics recognized as having expertise in the Treasury market, regarding the market for FRNs, the structure of the FRN, and models for pricing the FRN.

To assess the reliability of the data used in this study, including Treasury auction data and information on the largest holders of Treasury securities, we reviewed related documentation, conducted testing for missing data, outliers, obvious errors, and traced data from source documents, where possible and appropriate. To the extent possible, we also corroborated the results of our data analyses and interviews with other sources. Based on our assessment we believe that the data are reliable for the purposes of this report.

We conducted this performance audit from April 2013 to June 2014 in accordance with generally accepted government auditing standards. Those standards require that we plan and perform the audit to obtain sufficient, appropriate evidence to provide a reasonable basis for our findings and conclusions based on our audit objectives. We believe that the evidence obtained provides a reasonable basis for our findings and conclusions based on our audit objectives.

BACKGROUND

To achieve its primary debt management objective of financing the federal government's borrowing needs at the lowest cost over time, Treasury issues debt through a regular and predictable schedule of auctions across a wide range of securities. Most of the securities that are issued to the public are marketable, meaning that once the government issues them they can be resold by whoever owns them.[3] Marketable debt consists of bills, notes, bonds, Treasury Inflation-Protected Securities (TIPS), and, since January 2014, FRNs (see figure 1). Currently, Treasury issues bills with maturities ranging from a few days to 52 weeks; notes with maturities of 2, 3, 5, 7, and 10 years; bonds that mature in 30 years; TIPS with maturities of 5, 10, and 30 years; and FRNs that mature in 2 years.

Debt Management

Treasury issues securities in a wide range of maturities to diversify its portfolio and to appeal to the broadest range of investors. Issuing at multiple points across a wide range of maturity lengths both ensures high demand for Treasury securities and improves the general functioning of the financial markets by providing price transparency. Investors in Treasury securities include

- domestic private investors, such as individuals, banks, and pension funds;
- investment funds and asset managers;
- state and local governments; and
- foreign investors, including both private investors and foreign official institutions, such as central banks and national government-owned investment funds.

Treasury auctions securities on a regular and predictable schedule to reduce market uncertainty, facilitate investor planning, and enhance the liquidity of Treasury securities, thereby helping Treasury to borrow at the lowest cost over time.[4] Regular and predictable issuance means that Treasury debt managers choose the times and maturities of series of securities—rather than of individual issues—as part of their strategy for debt management. While this means that Treasury does not "time the market," issuing on a regular and predictable schedule does not preclude Treasury debt managers from considering fiscal conditions and the contemporaneous costs and benefits of shorter-term versus longer-term financing. Treasury also announces significant changes long before they are implemented and facilitates investor planning by giving market participants advance notice of its issuance plans through regular quarterly refunding statements. For example, Treasury published a notice and request for comments on its potential issuance of FRNs in March 2012, almost two years before the first Treasury FRN auction.

Total Federal Debt

Total federal debt consists of two components: debt held by the public and debt held by government accounts.

1. Debt held by the public
Debt held by the public represents federal debt issued by Treasury

---

> and held by investors outside of the federal government, including individuals, corporations, state or local governments, the Federal Reserve, and foreign governments.
>
> **2. Debt held by government accounts**
> Debt held by government accounts represents balances in the federal government's accounts (primarily trust funds, including the Social Security and Medicare trust funds) that accumulate surpluses.

At least in the near term, FRNs will constitute a small proportion of Treasury's debt portfolio. Treasury held its first FRN auction on Jan. 29, 2014, and it plans to issue the 2-year FRN every 3 months with a reopening auction in each of the 2 intervening months.[5] Treasury auctioned $15 billion at the first FRN auction in January 2014 and $13 billion at each of the reopening auctions in February and March. Assuming Treasury FRN issuance amounts remain constant, at the end of calendar year 2015 outstanding Treasury FRNs will total $328 billion, which is less than 3 percent of the current amount of debt held by the public.[6] The first FRNs have a 2-year maturity. Although Treasury regulations allow it to issue FRNs with maturities ranging from 1 to 10 years, Treasury has not announced plans to issue FRNs with other maturities.[7] The interest rate on Treasury's 2-year FRN is indexed to the 13-week Treasury bill and resets daily. Although the interest rate resets daily, in practice it will change only weekly because the 13-week bill is currently auctioned weekly. The 2-year FRN pays interest quarterly and accrues interest daily at a rate that equals the index rate from the most recent 13-week Treasury bill auction plus the FRN spread, which is determined competitively at the FRN auction (see figure 2).[8]

The mix of outstanding Treasury securities can significantly influence both rollover risk and the federal government's borrowing cost. Rollover risk includes two types of risk: (1) interest rate risk—the risk that Treasury will have to refinance its debt at less favorable interest rates, and (2) market access risk—the risks inherent in coming back to the market to refinance the debt.[9] As shown in figure 3, as of December 31, 2013, $7.9 trillion (or 67 percent) of outstanding marketable Treasury securities mature by 2019 and will need to be rolled over (i.e., refinanced)—potentially at higher interest rates.

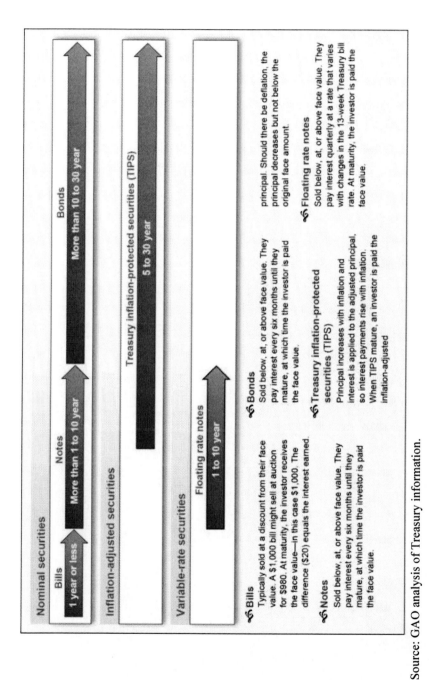

Source: GAO analysis of Treasury information.

Figure 1. Marketable Securities Offered By Treasury.

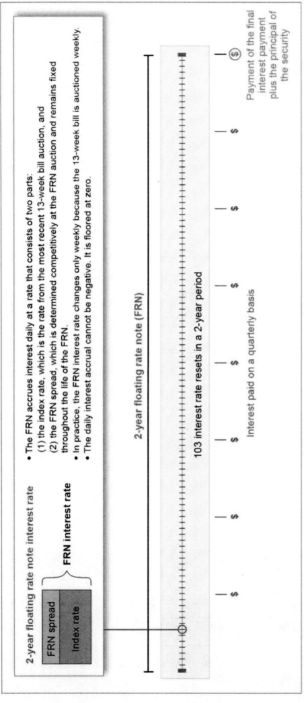

Source: GAO representation of Treasury information.
Note: Although the interest rate on the FRN is reset daily, the interest rate paid on the FRN will only change weekly because its index rate, the 13-week bill rate, is currently auctioned weekly.

Figure 2. Design Elements of the Treasury 2-Year Floating Rate Note.

Debt Management

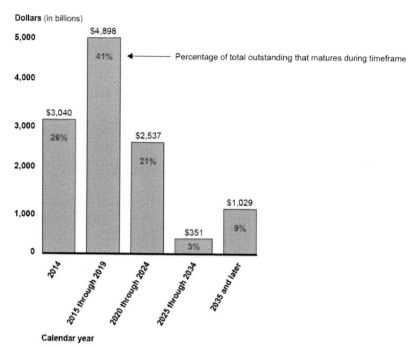

Source: GAO analysis of Treasury data.

Note: This includes only debt outstanding as of December 31, 2013. As Treasury refinances maturing debt, the dollar amount that will mature in subsequent times will increase. Included in this data is a small amount of marketable debt held by government accounts. This data does not include $15 billion of long-term marketable securities issued by the Federal Financing Bank and held by government accounts that are not currently traded in the market.

Figure 3. Marketable Interest-Bearing Securities by Year of Maturity, as of December 31, 2013 (Total Outstanding. $11.9 trillion).

One measure Treasury uses to manage rollover risk is the weighted average maturity (WAM) of outstanding marketable Treasury securities.[10] A high WAM could indicate that Treasury is paying higher rates on its debt because longer-term securities generally have interest rates higher than shorter-term securities. On the other hand, when they need to be refinanced, shorter-term securities expose Treasury to the risk of rising interest rates and market access risk. The introduction of the new Treasury FRN comes at a time when both interest rates and interest costs are expected to rise (see figure 4).

FLOATING RATE NOTES ARE LIKELY TO HELP TREASURY BORROW AT THE LOWEST COST OVER TIME, EXTEND THE AVERAGE MATURITY, AND INCREASE DEMAND, BUT THEY ALSO PRESENT CERTAIN RISKS

2-Year FRNs Are Likely to Cost Less than 2-Year Fixed-Rate Notes but Could Cost More or Less than Bills, and the Cost Will Vary by the Interest Rate Environment

We analyzed the potential cost to Treasury of issuing 2-year FRNs and found they are likely to have interest costs lower than 2-year fixed-rate notes and not substantially different than 13-week bills. As a result, FRNs will likely result in savings over the long run, helping Treasury achieve its goal of borrowing at the lowest cost over time. Our simulations found interest costs and savings varied depending on the security to which the FRN is compared, how the FRN is treated by investors, and the interest rate environment. We found that the cost of 2-year FRNs was generally less than that of fixed-rate 2-year notes, but that it could be either more or less than the cost of 13-week bills depending on assumptions regarding investor treatment of the FRN. In addition, in all cases and in all environments, savings tended to be greater—or added costs lower—under a model that sets the FRN spread based on its weekly reset than under an alternative model where the FRN spread is influenced by its final maturity of 2 years. We also found that, while issuing 2-year FRNs generally results in cost savings, they may be more costly than other alternatives in certain rate environments, such as rising rate environments.

Floating Rate Note (FRN) Spread

The difference (i.e., spread) between the index rate and the interest rate for the FRN. The FRN spread is determined at the FRN auction and is fixed over the life of the FRN.

Prior to issuance of the first FRN, Treasury conducted its own analysis of the potential cost of FRNs. Treasury's analysis found that from 1982 to 2010, issuance of 2-year FRNs would have led to cost savings compared to fixed-rate notes. Treasury's analysis, however: (1) compared the cost of 2-year

FRNs only to 2-year notes and not to other alternatives, and (2) assumed a fixed spread of 15 basis points (or 0.15 percentage points).

To estimate the potential cost of FRNs to Treasury, we compared the cost of hypothetical 2-year FRNs both to the cost of 2-year fixed-rate notes and to series of rolling 13-week bills, using historical auction data from January 1980 to March 2014 (see figure 5 below). We made these comparisons using two models, each with different assumptions about the spread over the index rate that Treasury would pay. We also compared the cost of FRNs in the various interest rate environments.

Floating Rate Note (FRN) Index Rate

The rate to which the interest rate of an FRN is indexed. Treasury's 2-year FRN is indexed to the rate from Treasury's most-recent 13-week bill auction.

Although it is uncertain what Treasury would issue in the absence of FRNs, Treasury has indicated that, at least initially, the FRNs would be a substitute for Treasury bill issuance. Both in interviews and in our survey of large holders of Treasury securities, market participants also indicated that they see the FRNs as a substitute for bills. However, Treasury has also indicated that it intends to reduce the share of debt funded by bills in order to increase its WAM. Without the 2-year FRN, Treasury might have increased the WAM by the same amount by instead increasing its issuance of 2-year fixed-rate notes, making them an appropriate benchmark with which to compare the costs of the FRNs.

Our analysis used two models for how the FRN spread—the spread between the index rate and the interest rate for the FRN—may vary over time. The FRN spread is set at auction and is expected to vary in response to changes in the level and volatility of interest rates. Because there is uncertainty about how market participants will price the FRN relative to other products, we considered two different models of the response of spreads to changes in different interest rates:

- A "maturity-based" model, where the spread estimate is influenced by the 2-year term of the FRN.
- A "reset-based" model, where the spread estimate is derived from the weekly reset term, which determines the nature of the interest rate risk faced by investors in FRNs.

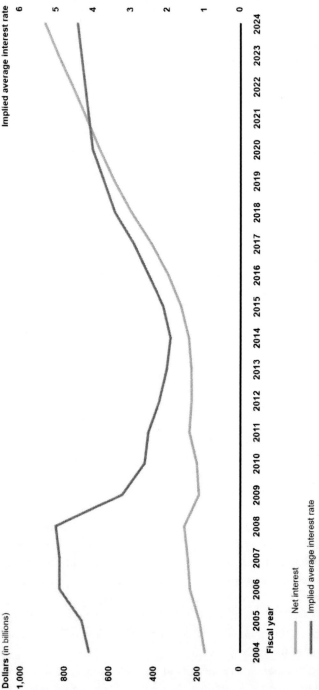

Source: GAO analysis of Congressional Budget Office data, including February 2014 baseline net interest payment projections.
Note: Actual values through the end of fiscal year 2013; projected values 2014-2024. Net interest outlays are interest expenses on Treasury debt held by the public and exclude other interest costs, including interest received by other federal entities, such as trust funds, and interest on debt issued by agencies other than Treasury (primarily the Tennessee Valley Authority).

Figure 4. Actual and Projected Net Interest Outlays and Implied Average Treasury Interest Rates, 2004-2024.

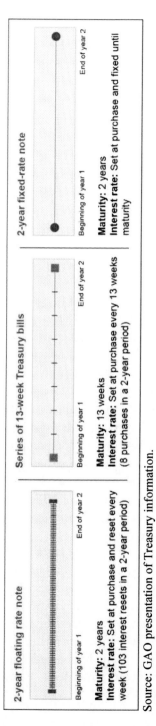

Source: GAO presentation of Treasury information.

Note: Although the interest rate on the FRN is reset daily, the interest rate paid on the FRN will likely only change weekly because its index rate, the 13-week bill rate, is currently auctioned weekly.

Figure 5. Three Different Approaches to Investing in Treasury Securities over 2 Years.

These two models are designed to approximate the range of potential spreads at which the 2-year FRN would have been expected to have been auctioned in historical interest rate environments. For more details on our models for FRN cost, including other models we considered, see appendix I.

Because interest rate environments vary substantially over time, we also compared how the cost of FRNs may vary based on changes in the level and volatility of interest rates.[11] Although these views are not generalizable, market participants and experts we interviewed expect the demand for FRNs to vary based on the interest rate environment. In addition, 58 of 62 respondents to our survey indicated that FRNs would be more attractive when interest rates are expected to rise; 49 of 62 indicated that FRNs would be less attractive when interest rates are expected to fall.

Costs of 2-Year FRNs Vary Based on What Treasury Would Have Issued Instead, Investor Treatment of FRNs, and Interest Rate Environment

We found that compared to 2-year fixed-rate notes, FRNs are likely to result in interest savings to Treasury regardless of how the FRN is treated by market participants; however, compared to 13-week bills, they could result in either savings or additional costs (see figure 6). Compared to 2-year fixed-rate notes, 2-year FRNs historically would have saved between $8.1 million in interest costs annually per billion in issuance under our maturity-based model, and $13.6 million under our reset-based model. Compared to 13-week bills, the FRN would have resulted in annual savings of $2.4 million per billion of issuance under our reset-based model but additional annual costs of $3.1 million per billion of issuance under our maturity-based model.

In addition to examining estimates of the relative savings and costs from issuing 2-year FRNs, we also analyzed the share of cases in our simulations where FRNs save or add to interest costs across different interest rate environments (see figure 7). We found that compared to 2-year fixed-rate notes, the 2-year FRN would have resulted in savings in 82 percent of cases under our reset-based model and in 72 percent of cases under our maturity-based model. Compared to 13-week bills, 2-year FRNs would have resulted in savings in 85 percent of cases under our reset-based model but added to costs in 81 percent of cases under our maturity-based model.

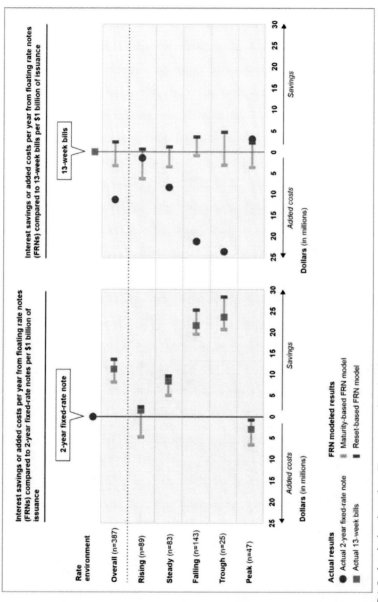

Source: GAO simulation based on Treasury and Federal Reserve data.

Figure 6. Interest Savings or Added Costs from 2-Year Floating Rate Notes Compared to 2-Year Notes and 13-Week Bills, by Rate Environment.

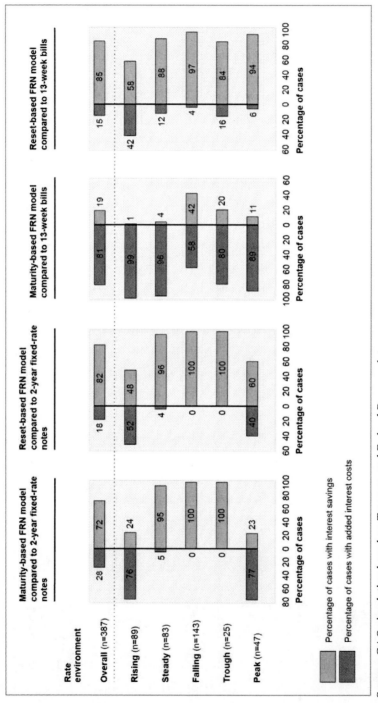

Source: GAO simulation based on Treasury and Federal Reserve data.

Figure 7. Percent of Cases Where 2-Year Floating Rate Notes (FRN) Save or Add to Interest Costs Compared to 13-Week Bills and 2-Year Notes, by Rate Environment.

We also found that the interest savings or added costs from 2-year FRNs varied with the interest rate environment regardless of how the FRN is treated or whether it is being compared to 2-year fixed-rate notes or 13-week bills. Relative to 2-year fixed-rate notes, FRNs tended to be more costly in rising rate environments compared to other environments. Compared to 13-week bills, FRNs tended to be more costly (in the case of our maturity-based model) or to produce less savings (in the case of our reset-based model). The extra cost or reduced savings in rising rate environments, however, tended to be less than the savings in steady and falling rate environments. As shown in figures 6 and 7 above, under our maturity-based model

- in rising rate environments, 2-year FRNs were less costly than 2-year fixed-rate notes in only 24 percent of cases and, on average, increased Treasury interest costs by 0.48 percentage points, resulting in $4.8 million in annual interest costs per billion in issuance; and
- in falling rate environments, 2-year FRNs were less costly than 2-year fixed-rate notes in all cases and, on average, reduced interest costs by 2.07 percentage points, resulting in $20.7 million in annual interest savings per billion in issuance.

We also analyzed the potential costs and savings from FRNs in environments with different levels of rate volatility and found that, at all levels of volatility, there was little variation between our two models. In periods of low, moderate, and high volatility, 2-year FRNs tended to produce savings compared to 2-year fixed-rate notes, but compared to 13-week bills, could produce either costs or savings, depending on which model is used. In periods of extreme (i.e., higher than "high") volatility, FRNs produced savings under both models. For more information on the results of this analysis, see appendix I.

Technical Demand May Increase Savings to Treasury, While a Liquidity Premium May Increase Costs

Factors other than interest rates may affect demand for FRNs, and Treasury could realize additional savings from FRNs due to these elements of technical demand. Both of the models we used to estimate the cost of FRNs assume the FRN spread is based solely on the relative value of FRNs compared to other Treasury securities. However, both our interviews with market participants and our survey responses indicate that demand for FRNs is also likely to be affected by technical factors, such as investment guidelines or

20   United States Government Accountability Office

regulatory requirements to hold certain types of investments. For example, Treasury officials and market participants told us that Treasury structured the FRNs in a way that makes them especially attractive to money market investors.[12] To meet investment guidelines and regulatory requirements, these funds tend to hold mostly short-term securities like Treasury bills and, because their interest rate resets frequently, FRNs.[13] These factors would create some technical demand for Treasury FRNs that is less sensitive to the relative value of the FRN. This generally would lower Treasury's costs since some investors would be willing to accept a lower interest rate at auction.

Technical Demand

Technical demand is driven by factors such as investment guidelines or regulatory requirements and is less sensitive to the relative value of the security.

Our survey results confirm that technical factors affect the attractiveness of FRNs for at least some investors. Twenty-seven of the sixty-two survey respondents said that FRNs' consistency with client or fund investment guidelines make them attractive to a great or very great extent. Results of our survey also show that 2-year FRNs are more attractive because they conform to regulatory requirements for certain sectors. Six of the seven money market mutual fund managers that responded to our survey indicated that conformance with limits on their holdings make the FRNs attractive to a great or very great extent. Similarly, five of the nine retail and commercial banks that responded to our survey indicated that conformance with new capital requirements made the FRNs attractive to a great or very great extent.

Treasury's costs could be increased if Treasury FRNs have a higher liquidity premium than other Treasury securities. Debt issuers, including Treasury, generally have to pay a liquidity premium on less liquid products— products that cannot be easily bought and sold in large volumes without meaningfully affecting the price—to compensate investors for the possibility that they might not be able to sell the security as readily as a more liquid product. A liquidity premium on FRNs that is greater than the premium on other Treasury securities could increase costs compared to our estimates. Although Treasury securities are generally considered very liquid and have very low liquidity premiums, market participants we interviewed said that FRNs might be less liquid than bills—Treasury's most liquid product—but more liquid than TIPS—its least liquid product.[14] FRNs are expected to be less

Debt Management 21

liquid than bills because (1) investors are more likely to buy and hold rather than to trade FRNs, and (2) FRNs are expected to have a smaller relative market size. Several market participants said that liquidity is likely to be lower initially and to improve as Treasury issues more FRNs.

Results of Initial FRN Auctions Were within the Range Estimated by Our Models

The results of Treasury's first three FRN auctions were within the range estimated by our models. At the first FRN auction in January 2014, FRNs were auctioned with an FRN spread of 0.045 percentage points. At the February and March 2014 auctions, FRNs were auctioned with discount margins of 0.064 and 0.069 percentage points, respectively.[15] The actual auction results appear linked to the spreads predicted by our reset-based model. In each of the three auctions, the actual auction results equaled the spread predicted by our reset-based model plus a small and consistent premium.

Mismatch between the FRN's Index Rate Maturity and Reset Frequency Poses Risk That Treasury Has Not Fully Analyzed

One element of the design of the Treasury 2-year FRN is that it is what the market refers to as a "mismatched floater." The difference (i.e., the mismatch) between the term of its index rate (13 weeks) and the length of its reset period (stated as daily, but effectively weekly) may introduce the risk of price instability on the reset date that is not typical of most floating rate securities. This is particularly the case if market participants treat the FRNs more like series of rolling 1-week bills. This might affect demand for the product in certain interest rate environments and, if so, could raise Treasury's borrowing costs.

For most floating rate securities, the maturity of the index rate and the frequency of the interest rate reset match. For example, a floating rate note indexed to the 3-month LIBOR—an interbank lending rate that is the most common index for non-Treasury floating rate notes—would typically reset every 3 months. Absent a change in the credit risk of an issuer, the value of a typical floating rate security returns to par—the value at maturity—at each reset. This leads to a higher level of price stability in floating rate securities compared to fixed-rate securities of the same maturity. This price stability is highly desirable to some investors.

> **Yield Curve Risk**
>
> The risk that interest rates at different maturity points—for example the rates for a one-week bill and a 13-week bill—will change relative to one another.

The Treasury 2-year FRN is different from a typical floating rate security in that it will reset every week to a 13-week rate. This mismatch introduces a tradeoff between yield curve risk and interest rate risk. Unlike a typical FRN, the price of the Treasury 2-year FRN will not reliably return precisely to par at each reset date before its 2 year maturity. This is because investors factor in changes between the 1-week bill rate and the 13-week bill rate. However, the price of the Treasury 2-year FRN should return close to par weekly, which is more frequent than if it had a 13-week reset. Treasury officials told us they believe that the frequent resets provide increased price stability for the FRN. They said that they expect investors to price the 2-year FRN in a way that reflects the expectation that the yield curve risk for Treasury's 2-year FRN is likely to be small relative to its reduced interest rate risk. However, if the difference between the 1-week rate and the 13-week rate changes substantially over the two year term, either in fact or in expectations, then the yield curve risk that the investor faces would be more substantial. It is possible that in higher and changing interest rate environments, the tradeoff between yield curve risk and interest rate risk may not be favorable to investors. This could be reflected in the spread, as investors bid for FRNs at auction in a way that compensates them for this additional risk, which could raise Treasury's borrowing costs.

> **Money Market Fund**
>
> A money market fund is a type of investment fund that is required by law to invest in low- risk securities. These funds have relatively low risks compared to other mutual funds and pay dividends that generally reflect short-term interest rates. Money market funds typically invest in government securities (including Treasury bills and notes), certificates of deposit, commercial paper of companies, or other highly liquid and low-risk securities.

Table 1. Effect of Floating Rate Note Design Features on Attractiveness to Investors

Feature	Effect on attractiveness of FRN			
	More attractive	Neither more nor less attractive	Less attractive	No basis to judge/ no opinion
Index rate maturity	24	28	6	4
Interest rate reset frequency	34	12	12	4
Difference between index rate maturity and interest rate reset period	16	34	7	5

Source: GAO analysis of survey data.

The mismatch between the index rate maturity and the frequency of the interest rate reset could have adverse effects on the costs of FRNs to Treasury. Treasury officials told us they discussed the design of the 2-year FRN both internally and with market participants and structured the 2-year FRN in this way for two reasons. First, as both those who commented on Treasury's proposal and Treasury have noted, the 13-week bill market is a large, liquid, and transparent market. Second, Treasury designed the 2-year FRN to meet high demand for short-term securities, and both Treasury officials and the market participants we spoke with cited the 2-year FRN's frequent reset as a reason for greater demand from money market funds. These funds face constraints on the average maturity of their holdings, which the weekly reset of the Treasury 2-year FRN helps address. This additional demand would likely result in lower costs and helps establish the new product for Treasury, which may outweigh the potential cost of the mismatch. Results of our survey show that overall, the FRN's index rate and the frequency of its interest rate reset chosen by Treasury—as well as the difference between the two— made the FRN more attractive to investors (see table 1).

Although Treasury officials told us they discussed the potential benefits and risks of the mismatch, Treasury had not analyzed how the mismatch could affect pricing. After we briefed Treasury officials on the issue in April 2014, Treasury began taking steps to study the mismatch to more fully understand its potential pricing risks. While its practice of regular and predicable issuance

24 United States Government Accountability Office

means Treasury issues all products in all environments, it is important that the risks of different securities are considered when making decisions about the mix of securities to issue. Treasury did analyze and consider how other design elements would affect pricing of the 2-year FRN and incorporated the results of that analysis into their final design. For example, Treasury analyzed how setting a minimum spread for the FRN would affect pricing. This analysis led Treasury officials to conclude that a minimum spread would unnecessarily complicate pricing, and it was excluded from the final structure of the FRN.

FRNs Can Help to Extend the Maturity of the Debt Portfolio, but They Make Treasury's Weighted Average Maturity an Incomplete Measure of Rollover Risk

Consistent with its goal of borrowing at the lowest cost over time, Treasury tracks and manages the average maturity of the debt portfolio. Relative to issuing bills, 2-year FRNs will help Treasury extend the average maturity of the debt portfolio, but only slightly. The effect that the FRNs will have on the average maturity is likely to be small because at least at the onset, FRNs are expected to constitute a small proportion of overall Treasury debt. Even so, Treasury officials said it is prudent to reduce Treasury's rollover risk by extending the average maturity. Treasury officials told us that FRNs will help Treasury continue to increase the maturity profile of the debt portfolio while meeting high demand for high-quality, short-term securities. Treasury could extend the average maturity of the portfolio by replacing issuance of shorter term notes and bills with longer term fixed-rate notes and bonds, rather than issue FRNs. In deciding what to issue, however, Treasury is confronted with making prudent decisions about investor demand by product. If Treasury issues the wrong mix of products, its overall cost of funding would increase, as investors would express their preferences in prices bid at auction.

Weighted Average Maturity (WAM)

The WAM of outstanding marketable Treasury securities is calculated by averaging the remaining maturity of all outstanding marketable Treasury securities, weighted by the dollar value of the securities.

Debt Management

> **Rollover Risk**
>
> Rollover risk includes two types of risk:
>
> 1. **Interest rate risk**
>   For a borrower, such as Treasury, interest rate risk is the risk of having to refinance its debt at less favorable interest rates and, for floating rate debt, of interest rates rising during the life of the security.
> 2. **Market access risk**
>   The risk associated with coming back to the market to refinance the debt. In times of federal budget deficits, maturing federal debt must be rolled over into new issuance.

Treasury tracks the WAM of outstanding marketable securities and publicly releases WAM data quarterly. Treasury debt managers do not have a WAM target, but over the past 30 years they have generally kept the WAM between 50 and 70 months (see figure 8). As of February 28, 2014, the WAM of the Treasury's outstanding marketable debt was 67 months, well above the historical average of 58.6 months. As of January 2014, Treasury continued to increase the WAM in a way that Treasury officials stated is consistent with their long-term objectives of financing the government at the lowest cost over time and ensuring regular and predictable management of the debt portfolio.

> **Marketable Debt**
>
> Marketable securities can be resold by whoever owns them. In addition to marketable securities, Treasury issues nonmarketable securities that cannot be resold, such as U.S. savings bonds and special securities for state and local governments.

Before Treasury began issuing FRNs, its WAM metric captured both components of rollover risk—interest rate risk and market access risk. Increasing the WAM by issuing 2-year FRNs instead of bills does not have the same effect on Treasury's risk profile that issuing 2-year fixed-rate notes would have. Since both 2-year securities have the same final maturity, they carry the same market access risk. The FRNs, however, carry a larger interest rate risk. The weekly reset means the interest risk on the FRN is similar to that of a 1-week bill, making it the shortest term product in Treasury's regularly issued portfolio from an interest rate risk perspective.[16] As noted above, it is uncertain what Treasury would issue in the absence of FRNs and whether 2-year FRNs will substitute primarily for 2-year fixed-rate notes, other fixed-rate notes, or bills. Relative to issuance of regularly issued bills, 2-year FRNs reduce Treasury's market access risk by locking in that funding for a longer period but increase interest rate risk due to the weekly reset.

As FRN issuance grows, Treasury's single WAM metric will remain a meaningful measure of market access risk; however it will no longer be an accurate measure of interest rate risk because floating rate securities carry higher interest rate risk than fixed-rate securities of the same term. Treasury debt management officials said that because Treasury issues in all interest rate environments and does not time the market, they primarily use the WAM metric as a proxy for market access risk in the portfolio. However, because market access risk and interest rate risk are related, Treasury understands the importance of both parts of the measure. Managing interest rate risk is an important aspect of Treasury's goal to borrow at the lowest cost over time; guidelines for sovereign debt management also emphasize the importance of managing the exposure of the debt portfolio to interest rate risk, as well as to market access risk.[17] Market participants that hold both floating rate and fixed rate debt use more than one measure to assess the length of their portfolios. For example, certain money market mutual funds are required to measure the average term of the fund in two ways—one based on the final maturity dates of the securities in the fund and the other based on the interest rate reset dates of the securities in the fund.[18] When we raised this issue with them, Treasury officials told us that they could easily publish another measure of interest rate risk.

FRNs Provide Treasury with Additional Flexibility in Its Debt Issuance

FRNs provide Treasury with additional flexibility in its debt issuance by adding a new type of security to Treasury's debt portfolio and by increasing overall demand for Treasury securities. If a new security brings incremental demand for Treasury securities, Treasury can grow its debt portfolio without increasing by as much as it might otherwise have had to the amount needed to finance the debt through existing securities. Our interviews and survey results found that although market participants will likely primarily purchase Treasury FRNs as a substitute for other Treasury securities (especially bills), market participants will also purchase Treasury FRNs as a substitute for other investment options, including FRNs from other issuers and repurchase agreements (see figure 9).

The results of the early FRN auctions indicate high demand for the security. The bid-to-cover ratios at the first three FRN auctions were higher than bid-to-cover ratios for other Treasury securities auctioned around that time. The first auction on January 29, 2014 had a bid-to-cover ratio of 5.67 and the reopening auctions in February and March had bid-to-cover ratios of 5.29 and 4.67, respectively. This compares to the bid-to-cover ratios in 13-week bill and fixed-rate 2-year note auctions averaging 4.53 and 3.37, respectively, over the same January to March period. According to Federal Reserve Bank of New York (FRBNY) officials, trading for the FRNs in the when-issued market was limited ahead of the three FRN auctions; nevertheless, the rates quoted in the when-issued market were very close to the auction results, an indicator that the auctions came very close to market expectations. This suggests that the price discovery mechanism of the market was functioning well for FRNs and that the market embraces and understands the security, which in turn indicates strong current and continuing demand that helps Treasury borrow at lower cost over time.

Bid-to-Cover Ratio

In a Treasury auction the bid-to-cover ratio is the dollar value of all bids received in the auction, divided by the dollar value of the securities auctioned.

Reopening Auction

An auction of additional amounts of a previously issued security.

When-Issued Market

When-issued trades are contracts for the purchase and sale of a new security before the security has been auctioned. When-issued trades settle on the issue date of the new security, when the security is first available for delivery.

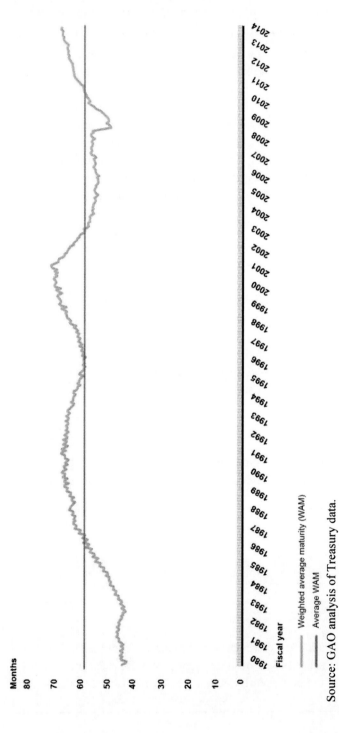

Source: GAO analysis of Treasury data.

Figure 8. Weighted Average Maturity of Treasury's Marketable Debt Outstanding.

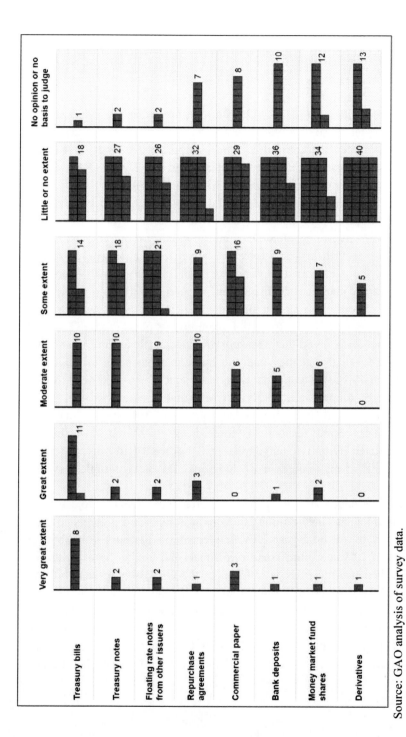

Source: GAO analysis of survey data.

Figure 9. Extent to Which Treasury Floating Rate Note Purchases Will Substitute for Other Investments, According to Survey Respondents.

Our survey results suggest demand for Treasury FRNs is likely to grow. Eighteen out of 61 survey respondents participated in the first Treasury FRN auction, but more said they plan to purchase Treasury FRNs this year. About half of all respondents (32 of 62) said their organizations definitely or probably will purchase Treasury FRNs in 2014.[19] Survey respondents anticipate that money market mutual funds, corporate treasuries, and foreign central banks are likely to have the most demand for 2-year FRNs. Survey respondents noted a number of reasons why Treasury FRNs are an attractive investment option, including the interest rate risk protection they provide the purchaser, their price stability, their use as a cash management tool, their consistency with investment guidelines and regulatory requirements, and the liquidity of the securities. The successful launch of a new type of security relies both on the readiness of investors and on Treasury's own operational readiness. Overall, market participants felt prepared for the introduction of a new security. According to almost all of the market participants we surveyed, Treasury provided sufficient information regarding its plans to issue FRNs (53 out of 62 respondents noted that Treasury provided sufficient information and the remaining 9 noted that they had "no opinion or no basis to judge.") In addition, of the 48 survey respondents that said that they would need to make systems changes to purchase FRNs, 36 said that Treasury or the Federal Reserve had provided adequate assistance or information to make the necessary changes. Some respondents noted that as of March 2014, they had not yet completed systems changes that will be needed to purchase FRNs. Demand for FRNs may increase as additional investors complete systems changes.

Although issuance of FRNs brings incremental demand for Treasury securities and demand in the initial auctions was high and is likely to grow, one design feature of the 2-year FRN may constrain Treasury's flexibility in the issuance of 13-week bills. Treasury officials and market participants both told us that because the FRN is indexed to the 13-week Treasury bill rate, Treasury will have to be more judicious in adjusting the size or timing of Treasury auctions of 13-week bills. As some comments on the proposed rule noted, there is some risk in indexing a floating rate note to a product from the same issuer. However, given that the 13-week bill is one of Treasury's largest and most liquid markets, its selection as the index rate minimizes this risk.

MARKET PARTICIPANTS IDENTIFIED OPPORTUNITIES FOR TREASURY TO ENHANCE INVESTOR INPUT AND EXPAND PRODUCT OFFERINGS

Overall Treasury's Communication with Investors Is Strong, but Certain Sectors Said It Could be Improved

As our prior work has found, communication with investors is essential as Treasury faces the need to finance historically large deficits expected in the medium and long term.[20] Overall, survey respondents said that Treasury provides sufficient information to investors on its debt management plans. Forty-three out of the 62 survey respondents said communication from Treasury occurred to a great or very great extent; no respondents said communication occurred to little or no extent (one had no basis to judge). In addition, most survey respondents said that they were able to provide sufficient input to Treasury, but respondents from some sectors reported lower levels of opportunity to provide input. The 26 respondents who reported opportunities existed to some or little to no extent included 10 state or local government retirement fund managers, 4 money market mutual fund managers, and 3 life insurance providers (see figure 10 below).

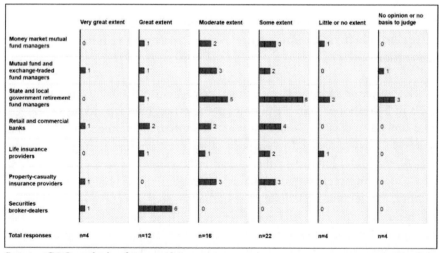

Source: GAO analysis of survey data.

Figure 10. Extent to Which Market Participants Said They Have Opportunities to Provide Input to Treasury.

To manage risks associated with borrowing, Treasury monitors market activity and, if necessary, responds with appropriate changes in debt issuance based on analysis and consultation with market participants. Treasury offers a number of ways for market participants to give input, such as providing comments on regulations solicited through the Federal Register and through the email box on the Treasury website. The Treasury Borrowing Advisory Committee (TBAC) is comprised of senior representatives from investment funds and banks and holds quarterly meetings to provide insights to Treasury on the overall strength of the U.S. economy and recommendations on debt management issues. In addition, FRBNY administers the network of primary dealers that also provide market information and analysis to Treasury. However, Treasury's Office of Debt Management does not meet regularly with all sectors, such as state and local government retirement fund managers. Survey respondent suggestions for improving communication with Treasury included administering surveys, holding regular meetings or calls with investors outside of the TBAC, polling investors on new product ideas, and providing a mechanism for submitting annual recommendations to Treasury from large investors. Without targeted outreach to all major sectors of investors in Treasury securities, Treasury could miss important insights to improve its debt management plans.

Survey Respondents Reported Interest Both in FRNs with Different Maturities and Other New Types of Treasury Securities

Responses from our survey of market participants indicate an interest in FRNs of both shorter- and medium-term maturities, but respondents expressed more limited interest in 7- and 10-year FRNs than in shorter-term FRNs (see figure 11). Survey respondents expressed the most interest in the introduction of a 1-year FRN. Interest in the 1-year FRN varied by sector, with mutual funds (including money market funds) expressing substantial interest in this maturity, while retail and commercial banks had little interest. Securities broker-dealers and state and local retirement fund managers expressed the most interest in FRNs with maturities other than 2 years, but other sectors— such as banks and property-casualty insurance providers—also showed some interest in these other securities. Treasury officials said they might consider issuing FRNs with longer maturities once both they and the market gain some experience with the 2-year Treasury FRN. Over the long run, Treasury FRNs with maturities other than 2 years are likely to provide a cost savings to Treasury relative to issuance of fixed-rate securities with the same maturity.

Survey respondents expressed their views on certain design features of FRNs with maturities other than 2 years. For instance, if Treasury were to issue FRNs with different maturities, almost all survey respondents (57 out of 62) thought those FRNs should also be indexed to the 13-week Treasury bill. More respondents said they would prefer daily interest rate resets to any other reset period for FRNs with maturities other than 2 years. Of the respondents who wanted new FRNs to be indexed to the 13-week Treasury bill rate, 13 would also prefer daily resets for all hypothetical maturities, including 4 state and local government retirement fund managers and 5 securities broker-dealers. Although this suggests that these respondents would prefer a "mismatched floater," as discussed earlier in this report, the mismatch feature may raise risks that result in higher costs to Treasury in certain interest rate environments. Additionally, respondents generally preferred quarterly interest payments for FRNs with other maturities and monthly auctions for 1-year and 3-year FRNs and quarterly auctions for FRNs with other maturities.

Survey respondents also expressed an interest in possible new Treasury securities. Suggestions were ultra-long bonds, callable securities, FRNs indexed to inflation, and zero-coupon notes or bonds (see figure 12).[21]

In addition, respondents suggested that certain debt management practices, specifically buybacks and reverse inquiry window, would enhance demand for Treasury securities.[22] However, respondents said that in general, changes to Treasury's current debt management practices—such as frequency of initial and reopening auctions, issuance sizes, and non-competitive award limits— would not enhance demand (see figure 13).

To achieve the lowest cost of financing the government over time, it is important that Treasury spread debt across maturities and take into account investor demand for new and existing products. The medium and long term fiscal outlook make evaluating the demand for Treasury securities, including new securities, increasingly important. Currently, Treasury feels unable to conduct a broad survey of market participants. For this reason, the insights on potential demand for new products from our survey can provide Treasury with a starting point so that it does not miss opportunities.

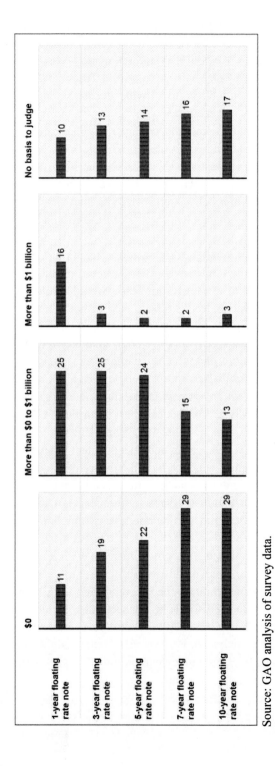

Source: GAO analysis of survey data.

Figure 11. Market Participants' Reported Estimated Purchases of Floating Rate Notes with Different Maturities.

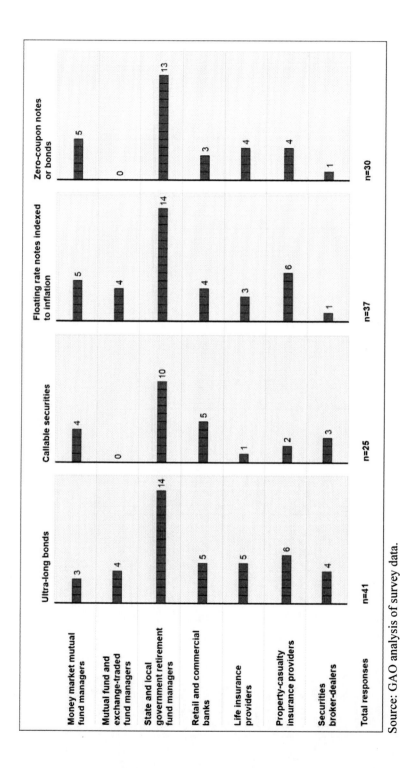

Source: GAO analysis of survey data.

Figure 12. Treasury Products that Could Enhance Investor Demand, According to Survey Respondents.

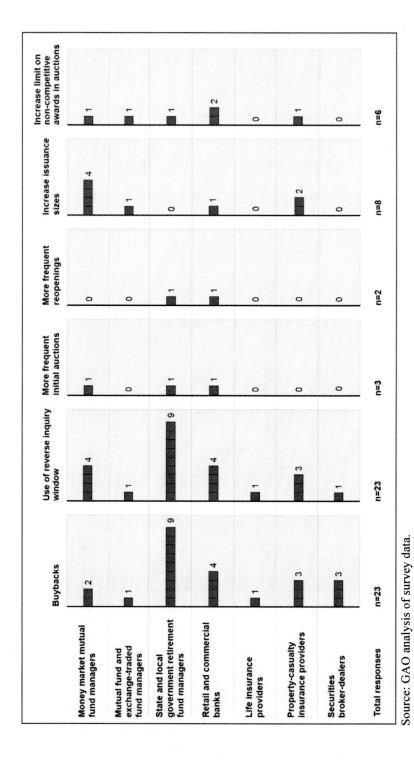

Source: GAO analysis of survey data.

Figure 13. Treasury Debt Management Practices That Could Enhance Investor Demand, According to Survey Respondents.

CONCLUSIONS

The U.S. Treasury market is the deepest and most liquid government debt market in the world. Nevertheless, Treasury faces challenges in managing the debt at a time when debt levels are high and projected to increase and when interest rates are also expected to rise. Given the market uncertainties and the federal government's fiscal challenges, increasing Treasury's flexibility to respond to changing market conditions in ways that minimize costs is prudent. FRNs are a tool that can help meet these goals. Over the long term, FRNs can reduce Treasury interest costs relative to fixed-rate securities that lock in funding for the same term. FRNs can also help enhance Treasury flexibility by marginally increasing demand for Treasury securities.

The design and implementation of FRNs has implications for Treasury's ability to minimize borrowing costs over time and for the balance of risks in Treasury's debt portfolio. Our cost analysis finds that in comparison to issuance of 2-year fixed-rate notes, Treasury is taking on additional interest rate risk but is likely to achieve interest cost savings while not increasing market access risk. The mismatch feature of Treasury's first FRN presents a tradeoff between different risks for both investors and Treasury that could raise Treasury's borrowing costs when interest rates are high and the yield curve is volatile. However, the mismatch also helps Treasury tap into the current high demand for high-quality short-term securities. Without analyzing how the mismatch between the frequency of the reset period and the maturity of the index could affect pricing, however, Treasury is unable to judge either (1) the risks (and therefore the ultimate cost) of FRNs in a different interest environment, or (2) whether the additional demand from money market funds due to the mismatch feature outweighs the potential costs it creates. A better understanding of these tradeoffs will be important when Treasury considers issuing FRNs with maturities other than 2 years. Furthermore, with the addition of FRNs to Treasury's debt portfolio, the weighted average maturity length of securities in the portfolio (i.e., the WAM) is now an incomplete measure of rollover risk because it does not accurately measure interest rate risk. Tracking and reporting an additional measure of the length of the debt portfolio that captures interest rate risk could help Treasury debt managers understand and weigh risks in the portfolio, and publicly reporting that measure would facilitate transparency and market understanding of Treasury debt management decisions.

Introducing FRNs at this time—when demand is high—can help Treasury and market participants become more familiar with the new security so that Treasury can expand to FRNs with different maturities if Treasury determines that doing so would enhance its flexibility and advance its debt management goals. It will also be important for Treasury to gauge market demand for FRNs and other products by soliciting input from all sectors of Treasury investors, specifically state and local government retirement fund managers. Such input can help inform Treasury decisions about changes to Treasury issuance or debt management practices that could enhance overall demand for Treasury securities. When deciding what to issue, Treasury must make prudent decisions about investor demand by product. If Treasury issues the wrong mix of products, its overall cost of funding will increase, as investors express their preferences in prices bid at auction.

RECOMMENDATIONS FOR EXECUTIVE ACTION

To help minimize Treasury borrowing costs over time by better understanding and managing the risks posed by Treasury floating rate notes and by enhancing demand for Treasury securities, we recommend that the Secretary of the Treasury take the following four actions:

1. Analyze the price effects of the mismatch between the term of the index rate and the reset period;
2. Track and report an additional measure of the length of the portfolio that captures the interest rate reset frequency of securities in the portfolio;
3. Expand outreach to state and local government retirement fund managers; and
4. Examine opportunities for additional new security types, such as FRNs with maturities other than 2 years or ultra-long bonds.

AGENCY COMMENTS AND OUR EVALUATION

We provided a draft of this product and the accompanying e-supplement (GAO-14-562SP) to Treasury for comment. On May 23, 2014 the Assistant Secretary for Financial Markets told us that Treasury thought it was an

Debt Management 39

excellent report, that they agreed with the recommendations, and that they had already taken steps to begin implementing them. For example, he told us that Treasury's new Office of State and Local Finance will bolster outreach to investors in the state and local sectors. Treasury also provided technical comments that were incorporated as appropriate. Further, Treasury told us they had no comments on the e-supplement.

Sincerely yours,

Susan J. Irving
Director for Federal Budget Analysis
Strategic Issues

APPENDIX I. SIMULATIONS OF FLOATING RATE NOTE COSTS

To estimate the potential cost of floating rate notes (FRN) to Treasury, we simulated the costs of 2-year FRNs based on Department of the Treasury (Treasury) auction data from January 1980 to March 2014 using two models, each with different assumptions about the spread over the index rate that Treasury would pay. We compared those costs to Treasury's actual costs of funding with 13-week bills and 2-year notes. We also analyzed how those costs varied over different interest rate environments.

Estimating Spreads

To estimate the range of potential costs from FRNs, we used two models of the costs of FRNs to Treasury:

1. A "maturity-based" model where the spread estimate is influenced by the 2-year term of the FRN.
   In the maturity-based model, the FRN spread—the difference between the index rate and the interest rate on the FRN—split the difference between the 13-week bill and 2-year note yields on the date of the FRN auction:

$$Spread_{FRN} = \frac{1}{2}\left(Yield_{2y\ fixed} - Yield_{Index}\right)$$

This model was suggested to us by a market participant as one way to estimate the likely spread for the Treasury FRN, and we found it to be reasonable.

2. A "reset-based" model where the spread estimate is derived from the weekly reset term, which determines the nature of most of the interest rate risk faced by investors in FRNs.

In the reset-based model, the FRN spread adjusted the yield of the FRN from the 13-week index rate to a yield equivalent to what a 1-week bill would provide. We imputed a 1-week bill rate based on a straight-line extension of the 13-week bill and 26-week bill rates on the date of the FRN auction. Where possible, we used the Constant Maturity Treasuries (CMT) series issued by the Board of Governors of the Federal Reserve System, which calculates rates for 13- and 26-week bills on a daily basis using secondary market data. However, the CMT series only begins in 1982, so for our simulations in 1980 and 1981, we used the weekly Treasury auction data. Once we imputed the 1-week bill rate, we subtracted the current index rate to compute the predicted spread:

$$Spread_{FRN} = -\frac{12}{13}\left(Yield_{26w} - Yield_{13w}\right) + Yield_{13w} - Yield_{Index}$$

This frequently results in a negative FRN spread, meaning that, under this model, the FRN generally has a yield lower than a 13-week bill. We allowed for negative spreads under this model because Treasury regulations allow the FRN to auction with a negative spread and, in very low interest rate environments, short term bills on the secondary market have sometimes traded with a negative yield.

While we considered other models for determining the cost of FRNs, these two models are designed to approximate the range of potential spreads Treasury's 2-year FRN would be expected to have been auctioned at in historical interest rate environments. We also considered models based on:

- **FRNs from government-sponsored enterprises (GSEs).** Several market participants we spoke with indicated that FRNs issued by

Fannie Mae and Freddie Mac would be the closest comparison for Treasury FRNs. However, we determined that GSE FRNs were not sufficiently comparable for our purposes due to the issuance practices and FRN structures used by Fannie Mae and Freddie Mac.

- **Swap prices.** Several market participants also suggested interest rate and asset swaps could be used to estimate spreads on Treasury FRNs. We reviewed results of simulations of FRN spreads published by one market participant, and found the estimates from this model usually to be within our own estimates for the FRN spread.
- **Theoretically derived formula.** We explored modifying the formulas used in Don Smith's "Negative Duration: The Odd Case of GMAC's Floating-Rate Note" to derive a theoretically correct spread price.[23] This approach predicted FRN spreads comparatively very close to zero and which generally lie within the costs predicted by the maturity-and reset-based models. This pricing model did not incorporate the pricing consequences of the mismatch between the reset rate and the maturity of the index, and so does not fully capture the pricing risks faced by the FRN.

Defining Interest Rate Environments

Because interest rate environments vary substantially over time, we compared the relative costs of the FRNs in various interest rate environments. The different environments, as used in our analysis and discussed in our report, are described below (see table 2).

To determine the trend of 13-week yields over a two year period, we estimated a linear time trend on the first difference of weekly yields (where t is an index of the number of weeks since the start of the two-year window):

$$Yield_{t+1} - Yield_t = \alpha + \beta * t$$

This is essentially equivalent to fitting a second degree polynomial to the yields, allowing us to capture changes in direction of the interest rate trend (i.e., peaks and troughs) as well as the slope of a linear trend. The estimated curves were used in classifying the interest rate environments.

The cut-offs for assigning an interest rate trend to a category of rising or falling—versus steady—were based on our professional judgment. Other approaches—such as using traditional statistical significance tests— conflate volatility with assessment of the presence of a trend and therefore are not appropriate for this determination.

We were able to use a data-derived approach to assign 2-year periods to our volatility categories. We use the RMSE statistic as an aggregate measure of the weekly yields' total deviation from the trend. We then used a k-mean cluster analysis to divide the sample into four volatility groups: low, moderate, high, and extreme.

Estimating Interest Costs

Using the maturity- and reset-based models, we estimated what the spread would be for FRNs auctioned on the same day as actual 2-year fixed-rate notes from January 1980 to March 2012, resulting in 387 simulated FRNs. We then applied these estimated spreads to the actual weekly 13-week bill auctions from January 1980 to March 2014, and calculated what the total interest cost would have been for each simulated FRN during this period. Like the actual 2-year FRN, we used a floor of zero for the daily interest accrual of our simulated FRNs.

To determine the relative interest cost of the FRN, we compared the estimated costs of the simulated FRNs to the costs of the actual 2-year fixed-rate notes and a rolling series of 13-week bills for each 2-year period. We estimated the average interest costs relative to 2-year notes and 13-week bills as well as the percent of cases where FRNs generate savings or additional costs compared to bills or notes.

Results of Simulations of FRN Costs by Volatility in Rates

In addition to the results presented in the body of our report, we estimated the cost of 2-year FRNs by volatility of the rate environment. As shown in figures 14 and 15 below, we found that, at all levels of volatility, there was little variation between our two models. In periods of low, moderate, and high volatility, 2-year FRNs tended to produce savings compared to 2-year fixed-rate notes, but could produce either costs or savings compared to 13-week bills depending on which model is used. In periods of extreme volatility, FRNs produced savings under both models.

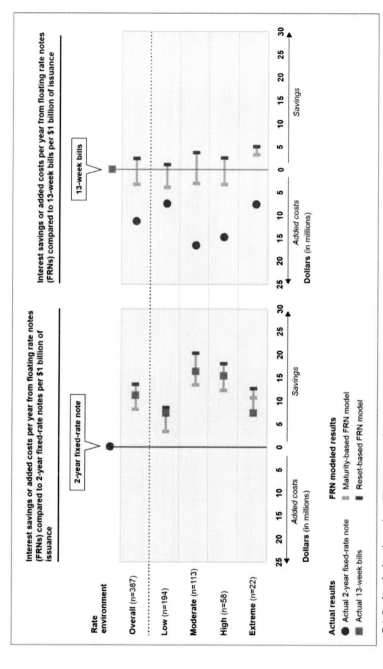

Source: GAO simulation based on Treasury and Federal Reserve data.

Figure 14. Interest Savings or Added Costs from 2-year Floating Rate Notes Compared to 13-Week Bills and 2-Year Notes, by Volatility in Rates.

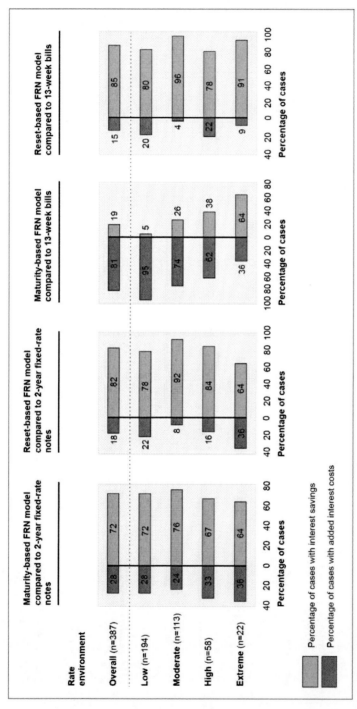

Source: GAO simulation based on Treasury and Federal Reserve data.

Figure 15. Percent of Cases Where 2-Year Floating Rate Notes Save or Add to Interest Costs Compared to 13-Week Bills and 2-Year Notes, by Volatility in Rates

Debt Management

45

Table 2. Definitions of Interest Rate Environments

Change in Rates	Rising	Cases where the trend of the 13-week bill rate increases by 1 percentage point or more over 2 years.
	Steady	Cases where the trend of the 13-week bill rate changes by less than ±1 percentage point over 2 years.
	Falling	Cases where the trend of the 13-week bill rate decreases by 1 percentage point or more over 2 years.
	Trough	Cases where the trend in interest rates initially falls, but then rises, over 2 years and where the trend in interest rates changes at least 0.5 percentage points in each direction.
	Peak	Cases where the trend in interest rates initially rises, but then falls, over 2 years and where the trend in interest rates changes at least 0.5 percentage points in each direction.
Volatility in Rates	Low	Cases where the root mean square error (RMSE) of 13-week bill rates in the sample is less than0.112.
	Moderate	Cases where the RMSE of 13-week bill rates in the sample is between 0.112 and 0.219.
	High	Cases where the RMSE of 13-week bill rates in the sample is between 0.235 and 0.500.

Source: GAO definitions using Treasury auction data.

APPENDIX II. SURVEY SCOPE AND METHODOLOGY

To address both of our objectives, we surveyed and interviewed market participants regarding (1) the market for FRNs, (2) the structure of FRNs, (3) other actions Treasury may consider to expand demand for Treasury securities, and (4) communication between Treasury and investors. To gather information from a broader range of investors, we administered an online survey to 82 of the largest domestic institutional holders of Treasury securities in the following sectors: money market mutual fund managers, mutual and exchange-traded fund managers, state and local government retirement fund managers, retail and commercial banks, life insurance providers, property-casualty insurance providers, and securities broker-dealers (see table 3). Results of the survey are not generalizable. For aggregate survey results reproduced as an e-supplement, see GAO-14-562SP.

Table 3. Survey Responses by Recipient Type

Sector	Total recipients of survey	Total completed surveys	Response rate (percent)
Money market mutual fund managers	9	7	78
Mutual fund and exchange-traded fund managers	10	8	80
State and local government retirement fund managers	26	19[a]	73
Retail and commercial banks	10	9	90
Life insurance providers	8	5[b]	63
Property-casualty insurance providers	12	7	58
Securities broker-dealers	7	7	100
Total	**82**	**62**	**76**

Source: GAO analysis of survey results.

[a] Three state-local government retirement funds refused to answer the survey; two specifically told us they fell outside the scope of our review.

[b] One life insurance provider refused to answer the survey.

To identify sectors for our sample, we reviewed data from the Federal Reserve's *Financial Accounts of the United States*, (table L.209, third quarter 2013) to identify which sectors have at least $60 billion in Treasury holdings. We excluded some sectors due to challenges in contacting certain entities, such as foreign monetary authorities, other foreign investors, and the household sector.

To identify the organizations within each sector that would receive our web-based survey, we used rankings of the largest organizations in each sector based on total assets or an equivalent financial indicator, such as assets under management or direct premiums written. From these ranked lists, we determined Treasury holdings for each organization and selected as many organizations as needed to represent at least 50 percent of the total amount of Treasury holdings for that sector (based on table L.209 of the Federal Reserve's *Financial Accounts of the United States*) or in the case of mutual funds, exchange traded funds, and money market funds, based on information from the Investment Company Institute on total assets under management in Treasury- and government-focused funds.

Debt Management

End Notes

[1] Total federal debt consists of two components: debt held by the public and debt held by government accounts. Debt held by the public is the value of all federal securities held by the public, i.e., investors outside of the federal government. Debt held by government accounts represents balances in the federal government's accounts—primarily trust funds, including the Social Security and Medicare trust funds—that accumulate surpluses. See GAO, "Fiscal Outlook: Understanding the Federal Debt," *Key Issues*, (Washington, D.C.: 2014), accessed Apr. 22, 2014, http://www.gao.gov/fiscal_outlook/understanding_federal_debt/overview and GAO, *Financial Audit: Bureau of the Fiscal Service's Fiscal Years 2013 and 2012 Schedules of Federal Debt,* GAO-14-173 (Washington, D.C.: Dec.12, 2013).

[2] Twenty-two banks and securities broker-dealers are currently designated by the Federal Reserve Bank of New York (FRBNY) as primary dealers and are expected to participate meaningfully in every Treasury auction by bidding for, at a minimum, an amount of securities representing their share of the offered amount (based on the number of primary dealers at the time of the auction). Primary dealers also have a role in making a secondary market for Treasury securities. (The secondary market is the market in which previously issued Treasury marketable securities are bought and sold among investors.)

[3] In addition to marketable securities, Treasury issues nonmarketable securities that cannot be resold, such as U.S. savings bonds and special securities for state and local governments.

[4] In a liquid market, trading can be completed at will and the offer and purchase prices differ only slightly. Liquidity is important to Treasury because investors are willing to pay more for liquid securities that can be easily traded, resulting in lower borrowing costs for Treasury.

[5] In a reopening, Treasury auctions additional amounts of a previously issued security. Reopened securities have the same maturity date and coupon interest rate or spread as the original securities, but have a different issue date and usually a different purchase price.

[6] Consistent with its practice for other securities, Treasury does not announce specific FRN offering amounts until shortly before each auction.

[7] 31 C.F.R. § 356.5(b)(3).

[8] The FRN index rate is the high rate from the 13-week Treasury bill auction converted to a simple-interest money market yield on an actual/360 basis.

[9] In times of federal budget deficits, all maturing debt must be rolled over into new issuances. Rollover risk also includes operational risk, such as the risk that a Treasury auction cannot be held due to technical problems with the auction systems.

[10] The weighted average maturity of outstanding marketable Treasury securities is calculated by averaging the remaining maturity of all outstanding marketable Treasury securities, weighted by the dollar value of the securities.

[11] Definitions of the interest rate environments we used can be found in appendix I.

[12] A money market fund is a type of investment fund that is required by law to invest in low-risk securities. These funds have relatively low risks compared to other mutual funds and pay dividends that generally reflect short-term interest rates. Money market funds typically invest in government securities (including Treasury bills and notes), certificates of deposit, commercial paper of companies, or other highly liquid and low-risk securities.

[13] 17 C.F.R. § 270.2a-7(c)(2).

[14] Previously, we recommended that Treasury take actions to increase TIPS liquidity; Treasury has implemented each of our recommendations. See GAO, *Debt Management: Treasury Inflation Protected Securities Should Play a Heightened Role in Addressing Debt Management Challenges*, GAO-09-932 (Washington, D.C.: Sept. 29, 2009).

[15] In a Treasury FRN auction, bids are made in terms of a desired discount margin. The highest accepted discount margin in the initial auction for a given FRN (which we refer to as the

FRN spread) becomes the spread for that FRN, and bidders pay the full value of the FRN. At subsequent reopening auctions of the FRN, the spread is fixed based on the results of the initial auction. Bidders at the auction still bid on a discount margin basis and may pay more, less, or the same as the full value, depending on whether the discount margin is less, more, or the same as the initial auction.

[16] Treasury issues 4-week, 13-week, 26-week, and 52-week bills on a regular schedule. Treasury issues cash management bills of varying maturities only as Treasury financing needs require.

[17] International Monetary Fund and the World Bank, *Guidelines for Public Debt Management*, as amended Dec. 9, 2003.

[18] 17 C.F.R. § 270.2a-7.

[19] These planned purchases include purchases at Treasury auctions, in the secondary market, and in the when-issued market.

[20] GAO, *Debt Management: Treasury Was Able to Fund Economic Stabilization and Recovery Expenditures in a Short Period of Time, but Debt Management Challenges Remain*, GAO-10-498 (Washington, D.C.: May 18, 2010).

[21] Ultra-long bonds are issued with a maturity greater than Treasury's current offerings, such as 40-, 50- or 100-years. Callable bonds are bonds that can be redeemed or paid off by the issuer prior to the bond's maturity date. FRNs indexed to inflation are floating rate notes that adjust the coupon rate for inflation while the principal is held constant. Zero-coupon bonds are bonds that do not pay interest during the life of the bonds. Zero-coupon bonds pay a lump sum, equal to the initial investment plus imputed interest, at maturity.

[22] Buybacks are the redemption of marketable securities prior to their maturity dates. We previously recommended that Treasury build the capacity for a buyback program that could be used to respond to potential changes in market conditions during times of deficit. This recommendation has not been implemented to date. See GAO, *Debt Management: Buybacks Can Enhance Treasury's Capacity to Manage under Changing Market Conditions*, GAO-12-314 (Washington, D.C.: Mar. 7, 2012). A reverse inquiry window is a method of purchasing securities where an investor consults with a broker-dealer who proposes to an issuer that a specific security be issued to meet the investor's needs.

[23] D. J. Smith, "Negative Duration: The Odd Case of GMAC's Floating-Rate Note," *Journal of Applied Finance*, vol. 16, no. 2 (2006).

In: Floating Rate Notes
Editor: Rosalyn Mercer

ISBN: 978-1-63463-214-0
© 2014 Nova Science Publishers, Inc.

Chapter 2

HOW TREASURY ISSUES DEBT[*]

Mindy R. Levit

SUMMARY

The U.S. Department of the Treasury (Treasury), among other roles, manages the country's debt. The primary objective of Treasury's debt management strategy is to finance the government's borrowing needs at the lowest cost over time. To accomplish this Treasury adheres to three principles: (1) to issue debt in a regular and predictable pattern, (2) to provide transparency in the decision-making process, and (3) to seek continuous improvements in the auction process.

Specifically, the Office of Debt Management (ODM) makes all decisions related to debt issuance and the management of the United States debt portfolio. When federal spending exceeds revenues, the ODM directs the Bureau of Public Debt (BPD) to borrow the funds needed to finance government operations by selling securities to the public and government agencies via an auction process. BPD manages the operational aspects of the issuance of Treasury securities, including the systems related to and the monitoring of the auction process.

During the mid-1970s, Treasury faced a period of rising nominal federal budget deficits and debt requiring unanticipated increases in issuances of securities. At that time, debt management was characterized by an ad-hoc, offering-by-offering survey of market participants. Due to the lack of transparency in such a process and the potential for market related volatility, a new strategy was implemented in order to provide

---

[*] This is an edited, reformatted and augmented version of a Congressional Research Service publication, R40767, dated August 18, 2009.

greater transparency and regularity to the debt management process. The purpose of this new strategy was to modernize the Treasury securities market, to realize the benefits of predictability in an environment of large deficits, and to use this predictability to induce policymakers to alter the practices of the institutions they managed. Treasury auctions became a key part of the new strategy focusing on regular and predictable debt management.

Most of the debt sold by the federal government is marketable, meaning that the securities can be resold on the secondary market. Currently, Treasury offers four types of marketable securities: Treasury bills, notes, bonds, and inflation protected securities (TIPS), sold in over 250 auctions per year. A small portion of debt held by the public and nearly all intragovernmental debt (debt held by government trust funds) is nonmarketable.

Investors examine several key factors when deciding whether they should purchase Treasury securities, including price, expected return, and risk. Treasury securities provide a known stream of income and offer greater liquidity than other types of fixed-income securities. Because they are also backed by the full faith and credit of the United States, they are often seen as one of the safest investments available, though investors are not totally immune from losses. Prices are determined by investors who place a value on Treasury securities based on these characteristics.

Legislative activity can affect Treasury's ability to issue debt and can impact the budget process. Congress sets a statutory limit on federal debt levels in an effort to assert its constitutional prerogatives to control spending and impose a form of fiscal accountability. The statutory limit on the debt can constrain debt operations, which, in the past, has hampered traditional practices when the limit was approached. The accounting of asset purchases in the federal budget has created differences between how much debt Treasury has to borrow to make those purchases and how much the same purchases will impact the budget deficit. If budget deficits continue to rise, thereby causing more resources to be devoted to paying interest on the debt, there will be fewer funds available to spend on other federal programs, all else equal.

INTRODUCTION

The U.S. Department of the Treasury (Treasury) performs three main duties, which are key to the functioning of the United States government and economy. Treasury manages federal obligations by collecting tax revenue and issuing debt when necessary. It also disburses payments of government benefits to eligible recipients. Finally, Treasury acts as a centralized account holder for other federal agencies. As part of these functions, Treasury also advises the President on economic and financial issues, works to maintain stability in financial institutions, and sustains economic growth. It accomplishes these goals by working with other federal agencies and foreign institutions.[1]

The Treasury, among other roles, manages the country's debt. The primary objective of Treasury's debt management strategy is to finance the government's borrowing needs at the lowest cost over time. To accomplish this Treasury adheres to three principles: (1) to issue debt in a regular and predictable pattern, (2) to provide transparency in the decision-making process, and (3) to seek continuous improvements in the auction process.

Specifically, the Office of Debt Management (ODM) makes all decisions related to debt issuance and the management of the United States debt portfolio. When federal spending exceeds revenues, the ODM directs the Bureau of Public Debt (BPD) to borrow the funds needed to finance government operations by selling securities to the public and government agencies via an auction process. BPD manages the operational aspects of the issuance of Treasury securities, including the systems related to and the monitoring of the auction process.

Recent economic instability and concerns over the long-term fiscal outlook of the United States bring prominence to the role of the Department of the Treasury in financing the obligations of the country. In addition, long-term obligations resulting from the retirement of the Baby Boom generation and rising health care costs, in the absence of policy changes, will likely lead to an unsustainable rise in future federal debt. Given these longer term challenges, the ability to maintain efficient and stable debt markets to ensure confidence and liquidity will remain an issue going forward.

As the amount of money owed by the United States to holders of Treasury securities rises, interest payments can become a greater burden on taxpayers. If investors choose to purchase Treasury securities, less money is available to finance other types of investments such as those in the private sector. To the extent that these securities are held by foreign governments or individuals abroad, those investors will be the beneficiaries of the interest payments.

Understanding how Treasury issues debt illustrates how this agency works to provide financial security and minimize costs incurred by taxpayers during a time of rapid debt issuance as well as addressing future concerns going forward. This chapter examines Treasury's debt management practices, focusing on the auction process, how prices and interest rates of securities are determined, and the role of market participants in the process. It also addresses the impact of debt on the federal budget.

AN OVERVIEW OF DEBT MANAGEMENT PRACTICES

Congress holds the authority to issue debt on behalf of the United States through power granted in Article I, Section 8 of the Constitution. This power was delegated to the Secretary of the Treasury in 1789. However, Congress retains ultimate control over spending, via the budget and appropriations process, and revenue levels, via tax legislation. If spending exceeds revenues, Treasury determines what type of debt instruments will be used to finance the borrowing.

The primary objective of Treasury's debt management strategy is to finance the government's borrowing needs at the lowest cost over time. Beyond providing financing to the federal government, the success of Treasury's debt management strategy also affects the global economy due to the influential role of the United States around the world. Treasury adheres to three debt management principles: (1) to issue debt in a regular and predictable pattern, (2) to provide transparency in the decision-making process, and (3) to seek continuous improvements in the auction process.[2] Adherence to this strategy is important to help secure growth and efficiency in both the domestic and global capital markets.

Development of modern debt management dates to the passage of the Second Liberty Bond Act of 1917, as amended, which designated the Treasury Secretary as the principal authority to determine the types of issues, terms, and techniques most appropriate to manage public debt. Prior to this measure, interest rates and maturity periods of bonds were set by legislation and Congressional authority.[3] Further refinements in debt management policy came when Treasury established the Bureau of Public Debt within the Office of Fiscal Service in June 1940. In the late 1980s, ODM, formerly known as the Office of Market Finance, became the central office responsible for the decision making behind Treasury's borrowings. The Bureau of Public Debt now oversees the operational aspects of the borrowing process of the federal government, accounts for and services federal debt, and provides reimbursable support services to federal agencies under the authority of the Treasury Franchise Fund.[4] It also conducts auctions of Treasury securities to allow individuals, institutions, and financial professionals to invest in Treasury bills, notes, bonds and inflation-protected securities (TIPS).

The Federal Reserve (Fed) works alongside the Treasury in the debt management process acting as Treasury's fiscal agent. Created in 1913 to institute stability in the banking sector following a time of financial panic, the Fed's role was primarily to oversee the money supply and supervise the banks during a time when the need for borrowed funds increased as the United States sought ways to finance World War I expenses.[5] For the first several decades of its existence, the Fed worked closely with Treasury to implement fiscal policy goals. Since the early 1950s, however, the Fed has operated independently from Treasury and uses its open market operations to manage the amount of money and credit in the economy via monetary policy. The Fed also provides banking services to the federal government by maintaining deposit accounts for Treasury, paying U.S. government checks drawn on the Treasury, and issuing and redeeming savings bonds and other government securities.[6]

HOW TREASURY SELLS DEBT

During the mid-1970s, the economy experienced a period of rising nominal federal budget deficits, which increased the level of debt issuance and resulted in market disruptions. At that time, Treasury decided that it needed to implement a new strategy in order to provide greater transparency and regularity in debt management.[7] The purposes of the new strategy were to modernize the Treasury securities market, to realize the benefits of predictability in an environment of relatively large budget deficits, and to use this predictability to induce policymakers to alter the practices of the institutions they managed.[8] As a result of the implementation of this regular and predictable schedule, Treasury was able to raise large amounts of money with a minimal impact on the financial markets. These policies also extended the average maturity of the national debt and produced a better defined yield curve.[9]

Auction Process

Auctions are the cornerstone of Treasury's regular and predictable debt management strategy.[10] Dates and offering amounts for each auction are scheduled and announced in advance. Bidders in Treasury auctions may be either foreign or domestic individual or institutional investors, or government entities at the federal, state, or local level. Treasury securities can be bought via a web-based account using the department's Treasury Direct system. Purchases of Treasury bills, notes, bonds, TIPS, and savings bonds can be made through this system.

The yield-to-maturity, interest coupon rate, and the discount or premium on a Treasury security are key terms in understanding the auction process. The yield-to-maturity is the rate of return anticipated on a security if it is held until the maturity date and is what is specified by a competitive bidder at the auction. The interest (or coupon) rate is set at the highest yield level, in increments of one-eighth of one percent, that does not result in a price greater than 100% of principal.[11] If the price of a Treasury security, as determined at auction, is less/greater than the face value of the security, then the security was purchased at a discount/premium.

Auction bids for Treasury securities may be submitted as noncompetitive or competitive. With a noncompetitive bid, a bidder agrees to accept the discount rate (or yield) determined at auction and is guaranteed to receive the full amount of the bid. With a competitive bid, a bidder specifies the yield that is acceptable.[12] A bid may be accepted in a full or partial amount if the rate specified is less than or equal to, respectively, the discount rate set by the auction.

Once the auction closes, all noncompetitive bids are accepted and competitive bids are ranked based on yield, from lowest to highest. Competitive bids are accepted, starting at the lowest yield, until the offering amount has been exhausted. The highest accepted yield becomes the "stop". A competitive bid will not be accepted if the rate specified in the bid is higher than the yield set at the auction. Though interest payments received by successful bidders may vary based on the yield specified in their auction bids, all securities in an auction are sold for a single price, computed based on the "stop" yield.[13]

Marketable Securities

Most of the debt sold by the federal government is marketable, meaning that securities are sold via the auction process and can be resold on the secondary market. Currently, Treasury offers four types of marketable securities, Treasury bills, notes, bonds, and inflation protected securities, sold in approximately 200 auctions per year.[14] If Treasury borrowing requirements or financing policy decisions change, the types of securities, the length of maturity periods, and offering amounts could be altered.

Treasury Bills

Treasury bills (T-bills) are short-term securities that mature in one year or less. T-bills are sold at a discount from their face value. The interest rate determines the discount from face value and the price paid at auction. When the bill reaches maturity, the investor receives the face value. T-bills are currently being offered with maturities of 4, 13, 26, and 52-weeks. Auctions for T-bills take place weekly on Tuesdays (4-week bills) and Mondays (13 and 26-week bills). Every 4 weeks, 52-week bills are auctioned on Tuesdays as well. The timing from the announcement of the auction, to its execution, to issuance of the purchased security is generally between 7 and 10 days.[15]

Treasury Notes

Treasury notes are interest-bearing securities, offered in multiples of $100, currently being offered in 2, 3, 5, 7, and 10-year fixed maturities. The relationship between yield to maturity and the interest rate determines the price at auction. If the yield-to-maturity is greater than/equal to/less than the interest rate, the price will be less than/equal to/greater than par (face) value. Treasury notes pay interest on a semi-annual basis and the investor receives the face value when the note matures. Treasury notes are currently being auctioned on a monthly basis (2, 3, 5, and 7- year notes) and quarterly (10-year notes).[16]

Treasury Bonds

Treasury bonds are interest-bearing securities, offered in multiples of $100, with maturities over 10 years. The price, yield, and interest rate of a Treasury bond are determined at auction in the same way as a Treasury note. Treasury bonds pay interest on a semi-annual basis and investors receive face value when the bond matures. Treasury bonds are currently auctioned quarterly. [17]

Treasury Inflation-Protected Securities (TIPS)

TIPS are interest-bearing securities that protect investors from inflation. TIPS are offered in multiples of $100, with maturity periods of 5, 10, and 20 years. The TIPS principal adjusts based on the movements in the consumer price index (CPI-urban, non-seasonally-adjusted) with a 3- month lag. These adjustments in the principal of the security form the basis for the interest payments, paid semiannually at a fixed rate. If inflation/deflation occurs, the interest payment increases/decreases. However, when a TIPS matures, the investor is paid the inflation-adjusted principal or original principal, whichever is greater. TIPS are currently being offered in April (5- year), January and June (10-year), and January (20-year).[18]

Nonmarketable Securities

Nonmarketable debt is composed of approximately 9% of publicly held debt and nearly all intragovernmental debt. Publicly held debt that is nonmarketable is primarily the state and local government series and savings bonds. [19]Intragovernmental debt is largely composed of debt owed by Treasury to the Social Security, Civil Service Retirement and Disability, and Medicare trust funds.[20]

The main purpose of publicly-held nonmarketable debt is to protect the bearers from market risk. The state and local government series was created in 1972 to restrict state and local governments from earning arbitrage profits by investing any tax-exempt bond proceeds in investments that may generate higher yields, thereby risking the returns. This program sells Treasury securities to state and local governments to help them comply with this requirement. Savings bonds provide a means for the small investor to participate in government financing. Savings bonds have been sold continuously since 1935 when they were introduced to encourage broad public participation in government financing by making federal bonds available in small denominations.[21]

U.S. government trust funds, which compose intragovernmental debt, contain revenues designated by law for a specific purpose. When revenues in the trust funds exceed benefit payments, the unspent monies must remain in the trust fund for future use. However, this excess cash is transferred to the Treasury's General Fund and is used to finance other activities which fall outside the specific purpose of the trust fund. In exchange, the trust fund is issued a Treasury "special issue" security to be redeemed at face value at any time in the future when the funds are needed.[22] "Special issue" securities are available only to trust funds and are designated as nonmarketable, earning interest on a semi-annual basis. The interest rate is determined by formula, based on the average yield of certain marketable securities.[23] Securities of this type protect the trust fund investments from market fluctuations.

Role of Federal Reserve and Primary Dealers

The Federal Reserve serves as Treasury's fiscal agent. In this role, it is responsible for the primary dealer relationships which are used not only for

Treasury auctions but other open market operations to conduct monetary policy. In addition, the Federal Reserve plays an important role in the operational aspects of the auction process and payments mechanism. The Federal Reserve is not responsible for making debt issuance decisions – this responsibility rests solely within Treasury's ODM to ensure the independence of the two institutions.

In addition, the Fed is a holder of Treasury securities. It is involved in the purchase and resale of these securities to the secondary market through its open market operations. These operations help keep the federal funds rate close to a target rate that is set by the Federal Open Market Committee. Its holdings of Treasury securities amounted to nearly $500 billion as of December 2008.[24] Any profits earned by the Fed through the sale of Treasury securities and other activities are remitted to Treasury and recorded as revenues in the federal budget.[25] The Federal Reserve banks also act as fiscal agents and depositories for Treasury accounts by accepting deposits of federal taxes and other federal agency receipts and processing checks and electronic payments drawn on the account.

The Fed's monetary policy actions can affect interest rates on Treasury securities in the short run. The Fed conducts its monetary policy by setting a federal funds rate, the price at which banks buy and sell reserves on an overnight basis, based on the supply and demand for bank reserves. Monetary actions by the Fed generally affect short-term nominal interest rates. If the Fed lowers the federal funds rate, resulting in a lower short-term interest rate, long-term interest rates are likely to fall also, though they may not fall as much or as quickly.[26]

Primary dealers are securities brokers and dealers who are registered to operate in the government securities market and have a trading relationship with the Federal Reserve Bank of New York.[27] Primary dealers are the largest purchasers of Treasury securities sold to the public at auction.[28] In many cases, auction purchases by primary dealers are later sold on the secondary or "when-issued" markets (see discussion in the next section).

In addition to their role in the auction process, the primary dealers also work closely with the Fed to execute its monetary policy. These primary dealers are large financial institutions who the Fed relies on to act as intermediaries through which Treasury securities are bought and sold and then resold on the secondary market in order to increase or decrease the money supply. They are expected to maintain trading relationships with the Fed's trading desk and provide the trading desk with market information and analysis that may be useful to the Fed in the formulation and implementation of monetary policy. The primary dealers also use this system to help them meet their liquidity needs by swapping securities with the Fed on an overnight basis. This type of securities lending has no effect on general interest rates or the money supply since it does not involve cash, but can affect the liquidity premium of the securities traded.

Other Purchasers of Treasury Securities

Along with the primary dealers and the Fed, individual investors, other dealers and brokers, private pension and retirement funds, insurance companies, investment funds, and foreign investors (private citizens and government entities) also purchase Treasury securities through the auction process and on the secondary market. Treasury releases a variety of data on purchasers of Treasury securities following each auction. The data are arranged into two categories. The bidder category data show purchases by primary dealers, direct bidders, indirect bidders, and noncompetitive bidders by bill type. The investor class data show purchases by different types of investors described in the previous paragraph.[29]

However, limitations on data do exist. For example, until a marketable security matures, ownership can change, meaning that the composition of ownership can be different from what it was at the time of auction. This is particularly true of primary dealers who purchase large amounts of securities and then resell them on the secondary market.

Secondary and Repurchase Markets

Participants in the secondary market play an indirect role in determining the price of Treasury securities. Once an auction is announced by Treasury, dealers and market participants start trading securities on a "when-issued" basis, meaning that once a security is purchased and issued, it will be immediately resold to the secondary market purchaser. Because trading starts in the secondary market before the actual auction takes place, "when-issued" market participants effectively determine the yield or discount rate of Treasury securities based on what they are willing to pay. [30]

Transactions of Treasury securities between investors and companies or dealers on the repurchase (repo) market play a role in the effective functioning of the credit markets. In the repo market, transactions take place between two parties who exchange Treasury securities, often on a very short term basis, for cash. The company or dealer pays the investor an agreed upon rate of interest for use of the funds with the expectation that the Treasury security will be repurchased at the mutually agreed upon future date. This process provides the company or dealer with the liquidity needed to meet immediate obligations.

Recently, the repo market has shown volatility as some investors were unable or unwilling to return the Treasury securities, thus affecting market liquidity. In the fall of 2008, failures in this market spiked to nearly $2.7 trillion, half of the market's total value, due to the general market panic caused by the bankruptcy of Lehman Brothers. These settlement fails were the highest ever recorded. Treasury took the unprecedented response of reopening four securities in October 2008 to renew market functioning.[31] In addition, the Treasury Market Practice Group, a private sector group sponsored by the Federal Reserve Bank of New York, suggested new guidelines to lower the level of future failures. Their recommendations resulted in the implementation of a three percentage point fee on failed repo transactions. However, since the interest rates on repo transactions generally remain close to the rates in the federal funds market, which are currently low, this fee may result in negative interest rates. Essentially, this means that investors will pay for owning the Treasury security that they have exchanged for cash and may be less likely to enter the repo market, potentially hurting liquidity.[32] Some analysts feared that that these negative interest rates will impact the broader Treasury security market, but, to date, volumes and trading activity remain robust.

MANAGING FEDERAL FINANCIAL FLOWS

The Secretary of the Treasury manages revenue, works to improve public credit, provides for on- time revenue collection and payment of debts.[33] If federal government finances are not correctly managed, financial stability and economic growth could be at risk. Throughout the year, the balance held by Treasury can fluctuate significantly as a result of higher or lower revenue collections or issuance of more or less debt during certain periods. As a result, Treasury must ensure that adequate funds are available, either via revenue streams or borrowing, to finance obligations. In order to finance the government's obligations while minimizing borrowing costs, Treasury must accurately project what cash requirements will be needed on a daily basis to cover government payments especially given these variations.[34]

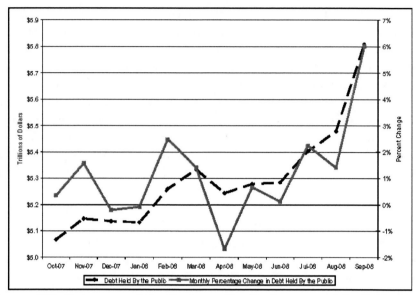

Source: U.S. Department of the Treasury, *Monthly Statement of the Public Debt*, October 2007 to September 2008, available at http://www.treasurydirect.gov/govt/reports/pd/mspd/mspd.htm.

Figure 1. Seasonality of Debt Held By the Public, FY2008

Treasury's financing needs generally follow a predictable seasonal pattern. Figure 1 shows the month-to-month growth in the public debt during fiscal year (FY) 2008. This varied from a low (or decline in debt held by the public) of -1.7% in April, due to the filing of personal income tax returns paid during that month, to a high of 6.0% (or increase in debt held by the public) in September, as a result of the need to meet obligations due at the end of the fiscal year.

The total amount of debt issued over the fiscal year depends in large part on the decisions made by Congress and the priorities it chooses in its annual budget and appropriations process. Recently, Treasury has issued increasing amounts of debt as a result of activities related to the economic downturn and resulting decline in tax revenues. Over the longer term, these priorities may change as the economy recovers and decisions on how to finance the promises to retirees for healthcare and other benefits may increase the demands on Treasury's debt issuance.

In addition to funding the needs of the government, Treasury manages the accounts of government agencies through the Financial Management Service (FMS). Loans are provided to Departments or Agencies in order to meet

How Treasury Issues Debt 61

obligations, such as payments owed to eligible beneficiaries of social service programs. FMS disburses payments to individuals and businesses, collects federal revenue, and issues government-wide financial reports.

How Much Debt is Outstanding?

Gross federal debt is composed of debt held by the public and intragovernmental debt. Debt held by the public, issued through the Bureau of Public Debt, is the total amount the federal government has borrowed from the public and remains outstanding. This measure is generally considered to be the most relevant in macro-economic terms because it is the amount of debt sold in credit markets. Intragovernmental debt is the amount owed by the federal government to other federal agencies, primarily in the Social Security, Medicare, and Civil Service Retirement and Disability trust funds, to be paid by Treasury.[35]

The Bureau of Public Debt and the FMS provide various breakdowns of debt figures. The most up-to-date data on federal debt can be found on the "Debt to the Penny" section of the Bureau's Treasury Direct website.[36] The Daily Treasury Statement (DTS) and Monthly Treasury Statement (MTS) provide greater detail on the composition of federal debt, including the operating cash balance, the types of debt sold, the amount of debt subject to the debt limit, and federal tax deposits.[37] The Monthly Statement of the Public Debt (MSPD) includes figures from the DTS as well as more detailed information on the types of Treasury securities outstanding.[38] The Office of International Affairs provides figures on the amount of debt held by foreigners through the Treasury International Capital System (TIC).[39] The TIC data reflect estimates of who holds Treasury securities at a given period of time, which may be different from who purchased these securities at auction.

Levels of federal debt change on a daily basis. On July 31, 2009, for example, gross federal debt totaled $11.669 trillion, intragovernmental debt totaled $4.334 trillion, and debt held by the public totaled $7.336. By the next business day, August 3, 2009, gross federal debt fell to $ 11.649 trillion, followed by $11.660 trillion on August 4, 2009.[40]

Treasury also estimates who owns federal securities. Because marketable Treasury securities can be and are often sold on the secondary market, ownership will change over time. As of March 2009, the latest period for which such estimates are available, gross debt totaled $11.1 27 trillion, of which, $4.785 trillion was owned by the Federal Reserve and

Intragovernmental Holdings. U.S. savings bonds accounted for $0. 194 trillion and foreign and international holdings accounted for $3.267 trillion. The remainder of the debt was held in depository institutions (i.e., commercial banks), pension funds, insurance companies, mutual funds, state and local governments, and other investors (i.e., individuals and corporations).[41]

FACTORS AFFECTING SUPPLY AND DEMAND FOR TREASURY SECURITIES

Investors examine several key factors when deciding whether they should purchase Treasury securities. As with all types of investments, price, expected return, and risk play a role in this process. Treasury securities provide a known stream of income and offer greater liquidity than other types of fixed-income securities. Prices are determined by investors who place a value on Treasury securities based on the characteristics of safety and liquidity afforded by this investment option.[42] Because they are also backed by the full faith and credit of the United States, they are often seen as one of the safest investments available, though investors are not totally immune from losses. The behavior of the market can lead to price changes, changes in interest rates, or inflation, which does create some investment risk. Despite the current economic conditions and financial market volatility, Treasury securities have remained attractive to investors.

Yield Curve

The yield curve shows the relationship between the interest rate (cost of borrowing) and the maturity of debt (i.e., U.S. Treasury securities) at a given time. In other words, the yield represents the rate of return an investor would earn if a security was held to maturity. The yield curve typically changes on a daily basis as interest rates move. Generally, yield curves are upward sloping (i.e., the longer the maturity, the higher the yield), with diminishing rates of increase over time.

Two opposing forces affect the slope and shape of the yield curve. First, investors must be compensated for choosing to invest now even though they may be able to achieve higher interest rates if they invested at a future point in time. This pushes interest rates up. Opposing this increase in interest rates is the fact that the longer the period to maturity, the greater the likelihood that interest rates will fall. This increases the risk to the lender (i.e., Treasury), as they could save on interest costs if they decided to wait before borrowing money. Generally speaking, the first effect will outweigh the second, leading to an upward sloping yield curve. An upward sloping yield curve also illustrates expectations for future economic growth and rising short-term interest rates. A downward sloping curve implies that investors expect short-term interest rates to rise above long-term rates.[43] These yield curves have frequently occurred before recessions.[44]

Yields can change for the same maturities from auction to auction and can vary on a daily (business day) basis. Treasury's Office of Debt Management generates the official daily yield curves to calculate a rate of constant maturity on Treasury securities in order to provide a meaningful measure of the yield on a security with a 10-year maturity, for example, even if no outstanding security has exactly 10 years remaining to maturity.[45] All securities with the same length to maturity must have the same yield, even if they were originally issued with different maturities or coupon rates. Yields are equalized through price changes.

Figure 2 shows the Treasury constant maturity rates for selected maturities since 1962. Rates on securities with different maturities generally track each other. This is because securities with similar maturity periods tend to have similar rates because they offer fixed interest payments over essentially the same period of time. Given that securities with longer maturities tend to reflect expectations about the future path of the interest rates of short-term securities, short-term rates generally provide a picture of the path of their longer-term counterparts. Therefore, over history, movements in constant maturity rates have generally tracked each other, regardless of length of maturity. [46]

Despite declines over the past year, long-term interest rates have recently begun to increase, approaching levels not seen since latter part of 2008 and generating some concern in the financial market. In June 2009 the rate on a 10-year Treasury securities briefly rose to nearly 4%, which is low by historical standards (as seen in Figure 2), but up from 2.5% in January 2009. The increase came in spite of the Fed's program to purchase Treasury securities in an attempt to keep interest rates low. At a June 2009 hearing before the House Budget Committee, Federal Reserve Chairman Ben Bernanke explained that the increase in Treasury and mortgage yields reflected other causes, including greater optimism about the economic outlook, a reversal of flight-to-quality flows, and technical factors related to the hedging of mortgage holdings.[47]

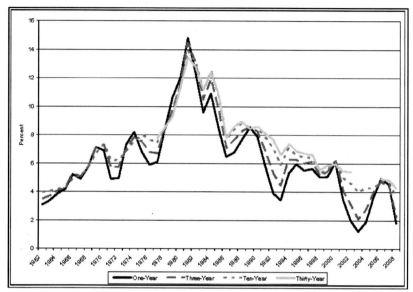

Source: Federal Reserve Board, *Federal Reserve Statistical Release*, H.15 Selected Interest Rates, U.S. Government Securities – Annual Series, available at http://www.federalreserve.gov/releases/h15/data.htm.

Notes: Treasury began issuing 30-year Treasury securities in February 1977 and did not issue these securities between February 18, 2002 and February 9, 2006. The Office of Debt Management also calculates constant maturity rates for securities with other maturity periods in addition to calculating rates for inflation-indexed securities (i.e., TIPS).

Figure 2. Selected Treasury Nominal Constant Maturity Rates (annual rates, 1962-2008)

Determining Maturity Mix

Newly issued Treasury securities, sold to finance the operations of the federal government, are offered at a mix of maturities in order to satisfy the provisions of the regular and predictable debt management strategy and to minimize interest payments over time. The profile of securities is also important due to its influence on liquidity. In addition, Treasury must make sure that it has adequate cash balances available to pay federal obligations. Balancing all of these objectives leads to a strategy which offers a mix of short- and long-term securities.

Longer-term securities generally command higher interest rates compared to shorter-term securities because investors demand greater compensation for incurring risk over a longer period of time. Generally, a strong economy will be accompanied by higher interest rates. If Treasury issues long-term debt during this time, they are committing to paying higher interest rates for a longer period and may decide to purchase shorter-term securities. However, this leads to uncertainties over the longer term, since the interest rate will likely change. During periods of economic downturn and low interest rates, Treasury may decide to finance at shorter maturities to take advantage of lower borrowing costs. This, however, may lead to more volatile and uncertain yearly interest payments because Treasury has to enter the market more often. Figure 3 shows the average length of marketable interest-bearing public debt securities held by private investors between 1969 and 2008, as of the end of each fiscal year.

Since 1969, the average maturity period of Treasury securities reached its minimum point in FY1976 at 31 months and its peak in FY2000 at 74 months. In the mid-1970s, prior to the initiation of the regular and predictable debt management strategy, the average maturity of Treasury securities declined due to the rapid increase in the deficit during FY1975. In order to meet the unexpected financing needs, numerous debt offerings took place. However, Treasury officials were generally reluctant to offer longer-term securities because they were unsure of investor demand. In contrast, during the surplus years of the late 1990s and the resulting decline in federal debt levels, Treasury did not have immediate financing needs and did not auction new securities as older ones matured. This effectively increased average maturity since more longer term bonds remained outstanding.

Despite recent increases in the amount of Treasury securities due to the federal government's economic recovery activities, average maturity of the debt continues to decline. Given the nature of current borrowing requirements, coupled with expected future demands on borrowing needs due to long-term obligations related to Medicare and Social Security, Treasury's Borrowing Advisory Committee recommended that Treasury increase the size of issues across the maturity spectrum in order to allow the Treasury to meet its financing needs over the short to intermediate term and reduce the uncertainty surrounding interest rates over the long-term.[48] Effectively, this should reduce risk and ensure adequate financing over the long term, while increasing average maturity.

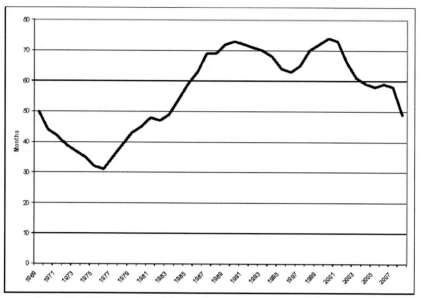

Source: Council of Economic Advisors, *Economic Report of the President*, January 2009, Table B-88, available at http://www.gpoaccess.gov/eop/tables09.html.

Figure 3. Average Maturity of Marketable Interest-Bearing Public Debt Securities Held by Private Investors, 1969-2008 (maturity period in months)

Current Economic Conditions

Current economic conditions as well as actions taken by the federal government to intervene in the housing and financial markets have raised concerns over Treasury's ability to raise money to finance obligations due to the large amount of funding needed. In order for Treasury to sell debt, buyers must have confidence in the value of U.S. currency and the ability of the government to pay back its obligations. In order to sell enough debt to finance spending in FY2009 and beyond, Treasury initiated more frequent auctions, new maturity terms, reopenings, and raised the overall amount of regular weekly and monthly securities issued. Further changes may be announced in the future.[49]

The new debt issued by Treasury will also face competition with debt being issued for similar purposes by other countries. With this competition, investor demand for U.S. securities may fall, at a time when issuance is relatively high, if foreign securities offer the prospect of better returns or are viewed as a safer investment. Alternatively, investors may decide to buy U.S. securities but only at higher interest rates if the market is flooded with supply, potentially increasing the cost of debt over the long term. The U.S. government faces a greater risk from competition because, compared to other countries, it has sold a relatively large amount of debt to foreigners. Despite this, demand for U.S. debt thus far had remained solid as indicated by the fall in interest rates.[50]

As a result of the Fed's actions during the financial crisis, there has been a large and unprecedented increase in the monetary base.[51] Though inflation levels remain low and are currently holding down interest rates, some investors have expressed concern that the Fed's actions will lead to inflation, thereby diluting the value of their investment, especially over the long term. If these fears become dominant, investors would demand a higher yield on Treasury securities.

BUDGETARY IMPACTS

Legislative activity can affect Treasury's ability to issue debt and can impact the budget process. The statutory limit on the debt can constrain debt operations, which, in the past, have hampered traditional practices when the limit was approached. The accounting of asset purchases in the federal budget has created differences between how much debt Treasury has to borrow to make those purchases and how much the same purchases will impact the budget deficit. If budget deficits continue to rise, thereby causing more resources to be devoted to paying interest on the debt, there will be fewer funds available to spend on other federal programs, all else equal.

Some economists have expressed concerns that long-term deficits could drive up interest rates, making it more expensive for the government, businesses, and consumers to borrow money. The government cannot add infinitely to the national debt without facing market consequences or hindering future ability to borrow. A portion of the current increase in the debt is attributed to financing the purchase of assets or loans to stabilize the financial sector. These investments are expected to yield some return in the future, while loans are expected be repaid, at least in part. In recent testimony to Congress, Federal Reserve Chairman Ben Bernanke warned that addressing the government's growing debt and annual deficits must begin or the country would risk facing further economic problems in the coming years. Though the country is dealing with rising levels of federal debt related to the current economic crisis, dealing with entitlement costs and related increases in the nation's debt as a result of obligations due to rising health care costs will likely become a concern once the economy recovers.[52]

Constraints of the Debt Limit

Congress sets a statutory limit on federal debt levels in an effort to assert its constitutional prerogatives to control spending and impose a form of fiscal accountability. At times, the debt limit has restricted the Treasury's ability to manage the federal government's finances. Standard methods of financing federal activities or meeting government obligations can be hobbled when federal debt nears its legal limit. If the limit prevents the Treasury from issuing new debt to manage short-term cash flows or to finance an annual budget deficit, the government may be unable to obtain the cash it needs. Because the law requires that the government's legal obligations be paid, the debt limit may prevent it from issuing the debt that would allow it to do so. While the debt limit has never caused the federal government to default on its obligations, at times it has added uncertainty to Treasury operations.[53]

Accounting of Recent Debt Increases

In 1990, the Federal Credit Reform Act (FCRA; Title V of P.L. 101-508) revamped the way that federal credit (direct loans and loan guarantees) was accounted for in the budget process. Prior to the creation of this law, asset purchases were recorded on a purchase price or net cash flow basis. If a subsequent sale led the government to recoup some of their investment, that would be recorded in a later fiscal year as negative outlays. Beginning in FY1992, asset purchases were recorded on an accrual basis, which reported the budgetary cost of a credit program equal to the estimated subsidy costs at the time the credit is provided. The subsidy cost was defined as "the estimated long-term cost to the government of a direct loan or a loan guarantee, calculated on a net present value basis, excluding administrative costs."[54]

Accounting under FCRA has become a more prominent issue due to recent federal financial interventions and resulting loans and asset purchases made by the federal government to stabilize the economy. Because the ultimate value of these assets once they are sold is not knowable, the ultimate increase in the federal debt as a result of these interventions is also unknown.

Asset purchases financed under the Troubled Asset Relief Program (TARP) require outlays equal to the purchase price, which increase the debt held by the public by the same amount. In the future, the government will likely sell the assets and the proceeds from the sale will return to the Treasury's General Fund.

However, the budgetary impact is somewhat different. The TARP law contained a provision which required budgetary accountability for these asset purchases to follow the provisions of FCRA with an additional adjustment for market risk. This means that for budgetary purposes, the cost of these purchases was recorded on a subsidy basis, which takes into account the asset's expected return. What the government paid to purchase the assets led to an increase in the debt held by the public, in the amount of the purchase price, that exceeded the increase in the budget deficit, the amount of the subsidy.

Interest and the Debt

Interest paid on the federal debt increases the overall cost of borrowing. Interest costs can be affected by various conditions, including legislative activity and the economy, as well as actions taken by the Treasury and the Fed, as discussed earlier. The level of budget deficits, hence the need to borrow, and federal debt can also affect the interest rates on Treasury securities. If interest rates are low, interest payments on Treasury securities may also be low, thereby making debt less costly. However, increased borrowing will increase the supply of Treasury securities, which generally leads to higher interest rates and future net interest payments.[55]

Despite the recent increases in federal borrowing due to federal financial interventions, stimulus legislation, and financial turmoil, the economic downturn and the actions of the Fed have kept interest rates near zero. Therefore, borrowing costs to the Treasury currently remain low. Interest payments are projected to match historically low levels both as a percentage of gross domestic product and as a percentage of total outlays even as overall debt is increasing. Over the long term however, borrowing costs are projected to grow, likely leading to increasing interest payments.

CONCLUSION

Part of Treasury's mission is to secure America's economic and financial future. In part, this is achieved by maintaining a regular and predictable debt management strategy as well as ensuring global trust and confidence in U.S. currency. However, Treasury's actions are affected by several outside actors, including Congress, the Fed, and different types of investors, as well as economic conditions. As long as the United States continues to issue Treasury securities to finance government operations, the actions of the Treasury will continue to play a key role in maintaining stability in the financial and credit markets and the U.S. economy.

End Notes

[1] U.S. Department of the Treasury, "Duties & Functions of the U.S. Department of the Treasury," available at http://www.treas.gov/education/duties/.

[2] U.S. Department of the Treasury, Office of Domestic Finance, Office of Debt Management Overview, available at http://www.treas.gov/offices/domestic-finance/debt-management

[3] Tilford C. Gaines, *Techniques of Treasury Debt Management* (New York: The Free Press of Glencoe, 1962), pp. 19, 21, 154.

[4] The Treasury Franchise Fund provides common administrative support services to other parts of Treasury as well as other government agencies on a competitive and fully cost-reimbursable basis. The collection of delinquent debt owed to the U.S. government is collected by the Financial Management Service. Department of the Treasury, Bureau of Public Debt, *Strategic Plan: Fiscal Years 2009-2014*, available at http://www.publicdebt.treas.gov/whatwedo/ bpdstrategicplan09-14.pdf.

[5] The Federal Reserve Bank of Minneapolis, *Born of Panic: Forming the Fed System*, August 1988, http://www.minneapolisfed.org/publications_papers/pub_display.cfm?id=3816.

[6] History of the Federal Reserve, available at http://www.federalreserveeducation.org/fed101/history/. For more information, see CRS Report RS20826, *Structure and Functions of The Federal Reserve System*, by Pauline Smale.

[7] Previously, debt was issued on an offering-by-offering survey of the market, whereby Treasury officials made decisions on what type of maturities to offer and when they should be offered based on anticipated needs. Auctions were used during this time for certain types of securities and some predictability did exist.

[8] Treasury bills had been issued on a regular basis for decades. With the new strategy, Treasury began issuing notes and bonds on a schedule as well. Garbade, Kenneth D., *The Emergence of "Regular and Predictable" as a Treasury Debt Management Strategy*, FRBNY Economic Policy Review, March 2007, pp. 54-55.

[9] Garbade, Kenneth D., *The Emergence of "Regular and Predictable" as a Treasury Debt Management Strategy*, p. 65.

[10] Though auctions were the main component of the new strategy, Treasury had tried to institute an auction based system in 1935 and 1963. Both of these earlier attempts failed.

[11] There are no coupon rates for Treasury bills – bills are sold on a discount basis.

[12] For bills and TIPS auctions, the bids are offered in terms of a discount rate rather than a yield.

[13] Garbade, Kenneth D. and Jeffrey F. Ingber, *The Treasury Auction Process: Objectives, Structure, and Recent Adaptations*, FRBNY Current Issues in Economics and Finance, February 2005, pp. 2-3.

[14] Cash Management bills are occasionally offered in order to meet short- and medium-term cash needs as determined by Treasury. These bills mature on dates determined by Treasury based on need, generally a few days from issue. Occasionally, Treasury also offers reopenings of previous auctions where additional amounts of a previously issued security are sold at the same coupon interest rate and maturity, but with a different issue date and price.

[15] U.S. Department of the Treasury, Treasury Bills, available at http://www.treasurydirect.gov/instit/marketables/tbills/ tbills.htm.

[16] Initial offerings of 10-year notes are currently auctioned in February, May, August and November. Each initial offer is followed by two reopenings of the same issue in January, March, April, June, July, September, October, and December. In a security reopening, the U.S. Treasury issues additional amounts of a previously issued security. The reopened security has the same maturity date and interest payment date as the original security, but has a different issue date and usually a different price. U.S. Department of the Treasury, Treasury Notes, available at http://www.treasurydirect.gov/instit/marketables/tnotes/tnotes.htm.

[17] Initial offerings of 30-year bonds are currently auctioned in February, May, August, and November. Each initial offer is followed by two reopenings in the two months following the initial auction. U.S. Department of the Treasury, Treasury Bonds, available at http://www.treasurydirect.gov/instit/marketables/tbonds/tbonds.htm.

[18] U.S. Department of the Treasury, Treasury Inflation-Protected Securities, available at http://www.treasurydirect.gov/ instit/marketables/tips/tips.htm.

[19] U.S. Department of the Treasury, Bureau of Public Debt, *Monthly Statement of Public Debt*, March 2009, Tables I and III, available at http://www.treasurydirect.gov/govt/reports/pd/mspd/2009/opdm032009.pdf.

[20] U.S. Department of the Treasury, Financial Management Service, *Monthly Treasury Statement*, June 2009, Table 6 – Schedule D, available at http://fms.treas.gov/mts/mts0609.pdf.

[21] Such offerings of Treasury securities dated back to 1776. Between 1776 and 1935, these securities were marketable and subjected the investor to market fluctuation. Particularly during World War I, small investors incurred significant losses if they were forced to sell their bonds prior to maturity.

[22] The trust funds now hold only special issues, but they have held public issues in the past.

[23] The specifications for securities issued to each type of trust fund are listed in separate places in the U.S. Code. Specifications for the Social Security Trust Fund can be found in 42 USC §40 1. Specifications for the Civil Service Retirement and Disability Fund can be found in 5 USC § 8348.

[24] Currency, not Treasury securities, is the Fed's primary liability. Treasury securities are assets to the Fed.

[25] For more information on the Fed's recent activities, see CRS Report RL34427, *Financial Turmoil: Federal Reserve Policy Responses*, by Marc Labonte.

[26] The federal funds rate is linked to the interest rates that banks and other financial institutions charge for loans – or the provision of credit. Thus, while the Fed may directly influence only a very short term interest rate, this rate influences other longer term rates. However, this relationship is far from being on a one-to-one basis since the longer term market rates are influenced not only by what the Fed is doing today, but what it is expected to do in the future and what inflation is expected to be in the future. For more information, see CRS Report RL30354, *Monetary Policy and the Federal Reserve: Current Policy and Conditions*, by Marc Labonte.

[27] A list of current primary dealers can be found at http://www.newyorkfed.org/markets/pridealers_listing.html.

[28] Purchases by primary dealers can be found at http://www.treasurydirect.gov/instit/annce result/auctdata/ auctdata_stat.htm.

[29] Auction results are available at http://www.treasurysecurities.gov/RI/OFGateway and http://www.treas.gov/offices/domestic-finance/debt-management/investor_class_auction. shtml. For an analysis of bidder category and investor class data, see Fleming, Michael J., *Who Buys Treasury Securities at Auction?*, FRBNY Current Issues in Economics and Finance, January 2007.

[30] Garbade, Kenneth D. and Jeffrey F. Ingber, *The Treasury Auction Process: Objectives, Structure, and Recent Adaptations*, FRBNY Current Issues in Economics and Finance, February 2005, p. 2.

[31] Data on Treasury fails back to July 1990 are available on the FRBNY's website at http://www.newyorkfed.org/ markets/pridealers_failsdata.html. Settlement fails are reported on a cumulative basis. For example, if a dealer fails to deliver $50 million in securities on the agreed upon date, but makes the delivery one day late, the fail is recorded at $50 million. However, if the $50 million is delivered 4 days late, the fail is valued at $200 million ($50m x 4). For more information, see Fleming, Michael J. and Kenneth D. Garbade, *Explaining Settlement Fails*, FRBNY Current Issues in Economics and Finance, September 2005.

[32] Fleming, Michael J. and Kenneth D. Garbade, *Explaining Settlement Fails*, FRBNY Current Issues in Economics and Finance, September 2005, pp. 4-5.

[33] U.S. Department of the Treasury, available at http://www.treas.gov/education/factsheets/history/act-congress.shtml.

[34] U.S. Department of the Treasury, *Strategic Plan: Department of the Treasury, Fiscal Years 2007-2012*, p. 15.

[35] For additional historical analysis of federal debt levels, see CRS Report RL34712, *Ebbs and Flows of Federal Debt*, by Mindy R. Levit.

[36] See http://www.treasurydirect.gov/NP/BPDLogin?application=np. Debt information typically lags the current business day by one to two business days.

[37] Current issues of the DTS and MTS, respectively, can be found at http://fms.treas.gov/ dts/index.html and http://fms.treas.gov/mts/index.html.

[38] The current issue of the MSPD can be found at http://www.treasurydirect.gov/govt/reports /pd/mspd/mspd.htm.

[39] Data on major foreign holders of Treasury securities by country is available at http://www.treas.gov/tic/ ticsec2.shtml#ussecs.

[40] TreasuryDirect, "Debt to the Penny" for July 31, August 3, and August 4, 2009, available at http://www.treasurydirect.gov/NP/BPDLogin?application=np

[41] U.S. Department of the Treasury, Financial Management Service, *Treasury Bulletin*, June 2009, Table OFS-2, available at http://fms.treas.gov/bulletin/index.html. For more information about foreign ownership of Treasury securities, see CRS Report RS2233 1, *Foreign Holdings of Federal Debt*, by Justin Murray and Marc Labonte.

[42] Dupont, Dominique and Brian Sack, *The Treasury Securities Market: Overview and Recent Developments*, Federal Reserve Board, Federal Reserve Bulletin, December 1999, pp. 792-793, available at http://www.federalreserve.gov/ pubs/bulletin/1999/1299lead.pdf.

[43] Federal Reserve Bank of San Francisco, *What is a yield curve, and how do you read them? How has the yield curve moved over the past 25 years?*, July 2004, available at http://www.frbsf.org/education/activities/drecon/answerxml.cfm?selectedurl=/2004/0407.ht ml.

[44] For more information, see CRS Report RS22371, *The Pattern of Interest Rates: Does It Signal an Impending Recession?*, by Marc Labonte and Gail E. Makinen.

[45] For information on the methodology used to calculate the constant maturity yields, see http://www.treas.gov/offices/ domestic-finance/debt-management/interest-rate/yield.shtml.

How Treasury Issues Debt

[46] Dupont, Dominique and Brian Sack, *The Treasury Securities Market: Overview and Recent Developments*, Federal Reserve Board, Federal Reserve Bulletin, December 1999, pp. 793-794, available at http://www.federalreserve.gov/ pubs/bulletin/1999/1299lead.pdf.

[47] U.S. Congress, House Committee on the Budget, *Challenges Facing the Economy: The View of the Federal Reserve*, 111th Cong., 1st sess., June 3, 2009., testimony available at http://budget.house.gov/hearings/2009/06. 03. 2009_Bernanke_Testimony.pdf.

[48] Report to the Secretary of the Treasury from the Treasury Borrowing Advisory Committee of the Securities Industry and Financial Markets Association, April 29, 2009, available at http://www.treas.gov/press/releases/tg111.htm

[49] U.S. Department of the Treasury, *February 2009 Quarterly Refunding Statement*, available at http://www.treas.gov/ press/releases/tg09.htm and *May 2009 Quarterly Refunding Statement*, available at http://www.treas.gov/press/releases/ tg1 10.htm.

[50] U.S. Department of the Treasury, Report to the Secretary of the Treasury from the Treasury Borrowing Advisory Committee of the Securities Industry and Financial Markets Association, February 4, 2009, available at http://www.treas.gov/offices/domestic-finance/debt-management

[51] For more information, see CRS Report RL34427, *Financial Turmoil: Federal Reserve Policy Responses*, by Marc Labonte.

[52] U.S. Congress, House Committee on the Budget, *Challenges Facing the Economy: The View of the Federal Reserve*, 111th Cong., 1st sess., June 3, 2009, testimony available at http://budget.house.gov/hearings/2009/06. 03. 2009_Bernanke_Testimony.pdf.

[53] For more information, see CRS Report RL31967, *The Debt Limit: History and Recent Increases*, by D. Andrew Austin and Mindy R. Levit.

[54] For more information, see CRS Report RL30346, *Federal Credit Reform: Implementation of the Changed Budgetary Treatment of Direct Loans and Loan Guarantees*, by James M. Bickley.

[55] For more information, see CRS Report RS22354, *Interest Payments on the Federal Debt: A Primer*, by Thomas L. Hungerford.

INDEX

A

access, 25, 26
accountability, ix, 50, 68, 69
accounting, ix, 50, 67
adjustment, 69
administrative support, 70
adverse effects, 23
agencies, viii, 14, 49, 50, 51, 52, 60, 61, 70
annual rate, 64
appropriations, 52, 60
arbitrage, 56
assessment, 6, 42
assets, 46, 67, 69, 71
auction data, vii, 1, 2, 5, 6, 13, 39, 40, 45
audit, 6
authority(s), 46, 52

B

banking, 52
banking sector, 52
bankruptcy, 59
banks, 7, 32, 47, 52, 57, 62, 71
base, 4, 53, 67
basis points, 13
beneficiaries, 51, 61
benefits, viii, 7, 50, 53, 60
bonds, viii, 6, 24, 25, 33, 38, 47, 48, 50, 52, 53, 54, 55, 56, 62, 65, 70, 71

BPD, viii, 49, 51
Budget Committee, 63
budget deficit, viii, ix, 25, 47, 49, 50, 53, 67, 68, 69
Bureau of Public Debt, viii, 49, 51, 52, 61, 70, 71
businesses, 61, 67
buyers, 4, 66

C

capital markets, 52
cash, 30, 48, 56, 58, 59, 61, 65, 68, 71
cash flow, 68
category a, 72
category d, 58
central bank, 7, 30
certificates of deposit, 22, 47
challenges, 37, 46, 51
citizens, 58
cluster analysis, 42
commercial, 5, 20, 22, 32, 45, 46, 47, 62
commercial bank, 5, 20, 32, 45, 46, 62
communication, 31, 32, 45
compensation, 65
competition, 67
composition, 58, 61
congress, 72
Congress, viii, 50, 52, 60, 68, 70, 73
Congressional Budget Office, 14

Index

Constitution, 52
consumer price index, 55
consumers, 67
cost, vii, 1, 2, 3, 4, 5, 6, 7, 8, 12, 13, 16, 19,
   23, 24, 25, 26, 27, 33, 37, 38, 39, 40, 42,
   49, 51, 52, 62, 67, 68, 69, 70
cost saving, 12, 33, 37
CPI, 55
credit market, 58, 61, 70
currency, 66, 70

D

debt management, vii, viii, 1, 5, 6, 7, 26, 31,
   32, 33, 37, 38, 49, 51, 52, 53, 64, 65, 70
debts, 59
decision-making process, viii, 49, 51, 52
deficit, ix, 48, 50, 65, 67, 68, 69
deflation, 55
Department of the Treasury, vii, 2, 4, 39,
   49, 50, 51, 60, 70, 71, 72, 73
deposit accounts, 53
depository institutions, 62
deposits, 57, 61
deviation, 42
draft, 38

E

economic crisis, 68
economic downturn, 60, 65, 69
economic growth, 51, 59, 63
economic problem, 68
economy, 50, 53, 60, 65, 68, 69
education, 70, 72
environment, viii, 12, 16, 19, 37, 42, 50, 53
environments, 2, 3, 5, 12, 13, 16, 19, 21, 22,
   24, 26, 33, 39, 40, 41, 47
evidence, 6
execution, 55
expertise, 6
exposure, 26

F

faith, viii, 50, 62
Fannie Mae, 41
fears, 67
federal agency, 57
federal budget, viii, ix, 25, 47, 49, 50, 51,
   53, 57, 67
federal funds, 57, 59, 71
federal government, vii, viii, 1, 4, 6, 7, 8,
   37, 47, 50, 52, 53, 54, 59, 61, 64, 65, 66,
   68, 69
Federal Register, 32
Federal Reserve, 3, 17, 18, 27, 30, 40, 43,
   44, 47, 52, 56, 57, 59, 61, 63, 64, 68, 70,
   71, 72, 73
Federal Reserve Board, 64, 72, 73
financial, 4, 7, 46, 50, 51, 52, 53, 57, 59, 61,
   62, 63, 66, 67, 69, 70, 71
financial crisis, 67
financial market(s), 7, 53, 62, 63, 66
financial reports, 61
financial sector, 67
financial stability, 59
fiscal policy, 53
fixed rate, 26, 55
fixed-income securities, viii, 50, 62
flexibility, 3, 26, 30, 37, 38
flight, 4, 64
floating rate notes, vii, 2, 3, 21, 38, 39, 48
fluctuations, 56
formula, 41, 56
Freddie Mac, 41
FRN, vii, 1, 2, 3, 4, 5, 6, 7, 8, 10, 11, 12, 13,
   15, 16, 18, 19, 21, 22, 23, 24, 26, 27, 30,
   32, 33, 37, 39, 40, 41, 42, 47, 48
funding, 5, 24, 26, 37, 38, 39, 60, 66
funds, viii, ix, 7, 20, 22, 23, 26, 30, 32, 37,
   46, 47, 49, 50, 51, 53, 56, 57, 58, 59, 62,
   67, 71

Index 77

G

GAO, vii, 1, 2, 3, 5, 9, 10, 11, 14, 15, 17, 18, 23, 28, 29, 31, 34, 35, 36, 38, 43, 44, 45, 46, 47, 48
global economy, 52
government payments, 59
government securities, 22, 47, 53, 57
governments, 7, 51, 56, 62
gross domestic product, 69
growth, 51, 52, 59, 60, 63
GSEs, 40
guidelines, 19, 20, 26, 30, 59

H

health, 51, 68
health care, 51, 68
health care costs, 51, 68
hedging, 64
history, 4, 63, 70, 72
House, 4, 63, 73
House of Representatives, 4
household sector, 46
housing, 66

I

improvements, viii, 49, 51, 52
income, viii, 50, 60, 62
income tax, 60
independence, 57
indexing, 30
individuals, 7, 51, 52, 61, 62
inflation, viii, 33, 48, 50, 52, 54, 55, 62, 64, 67, 71
initiation, 65
institutions, viii, 7, 50, 51, 52, 53, 57
interest rates, vii, 2, 3, 4, 5, 8, 11, 13, 16, 19, 22, 25, 37, 45, 51, 52, 57, 58, 59, 62, 63, 65, 67, 69, 71
intermediaries, 57
International Monetary Fund, 48

investment(s), viii, 7, 19, 20, 22, 27, 30, 32, 47, 48, 50, 51, 56, 58, 62, 67, 68
investors, vii, viii, 1, 2, 3, 4, 5, 7, 12, 13, 20, 21, 22, 23, 24, 30, 31, 32, 37, 38, 39, 40, 45, 46, 47, 50, 51, 53, 55, 58, 59, 62, 65, 67, 70, 71
issues, vii, 1, 6, 7, 21, 24, 25, 26, 32, 38, 47, 48, 50, 51, 52, 61, 65, 71, 72

L

lead, 51, 62, 65, 67
legislation, 52, 69
lending, 21, 58
liquidity, viii, 7, 20, 30, 47, 50, 51, 58, 59, 62, 64
loan guarantees, 68
loans, 67, 68, 69, 71
local government, 3, 5, 7, 25, 31, 32, 33, 38, 45, 46, 47, 56, 62
long-term debt, 65
low risk, 22, 47

M

management, vii, viii, 1, 5, 6, 7, 25, 26, 30, 31, 32, 33, 37, 38, 46, 48, 49, 51, 52, 53, 64, 65, 70, 72, 73
market access, 8, 11, 25, 26, 37
Medicare, 7, 47, 56, 61, 65
methodology, 5, 72
Minneapolis, 70
mission, 70
models, 5, 6, 13, 16, 19, 21, 39, 40, 41, 42
monetary policy, 53, 57
money supply, 52, 57
MTS, 61, 72
multiples, 55

N

national debt, 53, 67

O

ODM, viii, 49, 51, 52, 57
Office of Debt Management, viii, 32, 49,
   51, 63, 64, 70
officials, 2, 3, 4, 20, 22, 23, 24, 25, 26, 27,
   30, 32, 65, 70
OFS, 72
open market operations, 53, 57
operations, viii, ix, 49, 50, 51, 53, 57, 64,
   67, 68, 70
opportunities, 2, 3, 5, 31, 33, 38
optimism, 63
outreach, 2, 32, 38, 39
ownership, 58, 61, 72

P

participants, vii, viii, 2, 3, 5, 7, 13, 16, 19,
   20, 21, 23, 26, 27, 30, 32, 33, 38, 40, 41,
   45, 49, 51, 58
policy, 51, 52, 53, 54, 57
policymakers, viii, 50, 53
polling, 32
portfolio, vii, viii, 2, 4, 5, 7, 8, 24, 25, 26,
   37, 38, 49, 51
potential benefits, 23
predictability, viii, 50, 53, 70
present value, 68
President, 50, 66
price changes, 62, 63
price effect, 2, 38
price index, 55
price instability, 21
price stability, 21, 22, 30
principles, vii, 49, 51, 52
private sector, 51, 59
professionals, 52
project, 59
protection, 30
public debt, 52, 60, 65

R

rate of return, 54, 62
recommendations, 2, 32, 39, 47, 59
recovery, 65
reform, 68, 73
regulations, 8, 32, 40
regulatory changes, 4
regulatory requirements, 20, 30
reliability, 6
repo, 58, 59
requirements, 20, 54, 59, 65
resale, 57
reserves, 57
resources, ix, 50, 67
response, 13, 59
retail, 5, 20, 32, 45
retirement, 3, 5, 31, 32, 33, 38, 45, 46, 51,
   58
revenue, 50, 52, 59, 61
risk(s), viii, 2, 3, 8, 11, 13, 21, 22, 23, 24,
   25, 26, 30, 32, 33, 37, 38, 40, 41, 47, 50,
   56, 59, 62, 63, 65, 66, 67, 68, 69
risk profile, 25
root, 4, 45

S

safety, 62
savings, 12, 16, 19, 25, 42, 47, 53, 56, 62
scope, 46
Secretary of the Treasury, 38, 52, 59, 73
securities, vii, viii, 1, 2, 3, 4, 5, 6, 7, 8, 11,
   13, 19, 20, 21, 22, 23, 24, 25, 26, 27, 30,
   32, 33, 37, 38, 45, 47, 48, 49, 50, 51, 52,
   53, 54, 55, 56, 57, 58, 59, 61, 62, 63, 64,
   65, 66, 67, 69, 70, 71, 72
security, vii, 1, 3, 4, 12, 20, 21, 22, 25, 26,
   27, 30, 38, 47, 48, 51, 54, 55, 56, 58, 59,
   62, 63, 71
services, 52, 53, 70
shape, 62
short-term interest rate, 22, 47, 57, 63

Index

simulation(s), 5, 12, 16, 17, 18, 40, 41, 43, 44
Social Security, 7, 47, 56, 61, 65, 71
specifications, 71
spending, viii, ix, 49, 50, 51, 52, 66, 68
stability, 21, 51, 52, 59, 70
state, 3, 5, 7, 25, 31, 32, 33, 38, 39, 45, 46, 47, 53, 56, 62
stimulus, 69
strategy, vii, viii, 49, 51, 52, 53, 64, 65, 70
structure, 5, 24, 45
subsidy, 68, 69
support services, 52, 70
surplus, 65
survey, viii, 49, 70

T

target, 25, 57
taxes, 57
taxpayers, 51
technical comments, 39
techniques, 52
Tennessee Valley Authority, 14
testing, 6
TIPS, viii, 4, 6, 20, 47, 50, 52, 53, 55, 64, 70
Title V, 68
tracks, 24, 25
trade, 21
traditional practices, ix, 50, 67
transactions, 58, 59
transparency, viii, 7, 37, 49, 51, 52, 53
Treasury bill(s), vii, viii, 1, 8, 13, 20, 22, 30, 33, 47, 50, 52, 53, 54, 55, 70
Treasury debt management, vii, 1, 5, 26, 37
Treasury Secretary, 52

Treasury securities, vii, viii, 1, 2, 3, 4, 5, 6, 7, 8, 11, 13, 19, 20, 24, 26, 27, 30, 32, 33, 37, 38, 45, 47, 49, 50, 51, 52, 53, 54, 56, 57, 58, 59, 61, 62, 63, 64, 65, 67, 69, 70, 71, 72
treatment, 12
trust fund, viii, 7, 14, 47, 50, 56, 61, 71

U

U.S. Department of the Treasury, vii, 49, 50, 60, 70, 71, 72, 73
U.S. economy, 32, 70
U.S. Treasury, 4, 37, 62, 71
United States, viii, 1, 46, 49, 50, 51, 52, 53, 62, 70
urban, 55

V

variations, 59
volatility, viii, 13, 16, 19, 42, 49, 59, 62

W

Washington, 47, 48
web, 46, 53
World Bank, 48
World War I, 53, 71

Y

yield, 22, 37, 40, 47, 53, 54, 55, 56, 58, 62, 63, 67, 70, 72